SCOTLAND

Text
Antony Kamm

Photography
Ronald W. Weir
Roberto Matassa
The Photo Source
Oxford Scientific Films
Highlands and Islands Development Board
Telegraph Colour Library
Scottish Tourist Board

Design
Teddy Hartshorn
Sally Strugnell
Alison Jewell

Editorial
Trevor Hall
Andrew Preston
Gill Waugh
Fleur Robertson

Production
Ruth Arthur
Pamela Simpkins
Joanna Keywood

Director of Production
Gerald Hughes

Director of Publishing
David Gibbon

Acknowledgement
The publishers acknowledge with grateful thanks the invaluable
assistance of Ronald J. Weir, Trina McLennan and Moira Campbell,
without whose contribution this book would not have been possible.

CLB 2172
This edition published 1990
ISBN 0 86283 672 7

SCOTLAND

Antony Kamm

Colour Library Books

The Peoples of Scotland

The first people to settle in the thickly forested northlands of Britain came in log canoes, in search of fresh hunting and fishing grounds, almost nine thousand years ago. In western Asia people had, by this time, learned to grow crops and to domesticate cattle, sheep and goats, but it was to be several thousand years more before these skills, and the communities who knew how to use them, filtered through into the region that is now Scotland.

Early Scottish agriculturalists were intrepid, as well as hardy. In about 3000 B.C., a band of them, with their families, cattle and sheep, embarked in rudimentary ferryboats and paddled away from the north coast. They missed out the island of Hoy, and landed at Skara Brae, on the west mainland of Orkney. Here, on the windswept shore, they constructed an underground village of slabs of stone, covering it over with turf and rubbish. The individual one-room homes had stone-flagged floors, stone bunks, stone cupboards and storage boxes, and drainage systems. In about 2500 B.C., possibly because of worsening weather conditions, the site was evacuated. Shortly afterwards, a storm buried it in sand. It remained unknown, silent, virtually intact, until A.D. 1850, when another storm blew away some of the clinging sand, revealing, now that it has been fully excavated, the best-preserved Stone Age village in northern Europe. The ingenious nature of this living complex is reflected in the chambered cairns in which the people of that time buried their dead, and which can be seen, in various stages of preservation, not only in Orkney and other parts of the Highlands, but on the isle of Arran and in Wigtownshire.

Agricultural land on the mainland had to be laboriously hacked, chip by chip, out of the forests and scrub. In about 2000 B.C., Bronze Age Celts came from Europe, bringing new skills, in particular the ability to make weapons, axes and farm tools from copper and from the equally sharp but tougher bronze (an alloy of copper and tin), and to craft jewellery of copper and gold. There were deposits of copper to be found in various localities, especially by Loch Fyne and Loch Ness, and around the Ochils and Leadhills; and gold by Loch Tay and Loch Earn, and in the far northeast. The nearest tin, however, was at the tip of Cornwall, or had to be brought from central Europe. Yet the early Scottish metal-workers got tin somehow, and in doing so became traders, exchanging for it local copper and gold.

Even more radical changes were on the way. In the Celtic homelands in the middle of Europe, another people had discovered how to mine iron ore and turn it into the most effective substance yet known. By controlling the texture in a furnace, and hammering the results into whatever shapes were required, they made swords and axe-heads, farm tools, and even the rims for chariot wheels, which were more effective and lasting than any before. Armed with their new and fearsome weapons, the Iron Age Celtic warlords fought their way across Europe and into Britain and Ireland during the fourth century B.C. They came to the northlands in about 750 B.C., settling as and where they liked. Their communities and tribes got from the land their means of existence, and exercised their aggressive tendencies on each other, now that there was no concerted opposition.

To protect themselves against sporadic raids and robber bands, the settlers built clusters of stone huts on hill-tops, surrounding them with defensive walls of timber and stone, which they dug out of quarries with their iron chisels, crowbars and sledgehammers. Other dwelling-places were less conventional. Where wood was plentiful and near a loch, ingenious house-designers built homes actually in the water. These round crannogs, constructed of wood and thatch, stood on artificial islands, with only a narrow causeway, hidden under the surface of the water, linking them to the shore. Less inventive, and much more vulnerable to attack, were earth-houses (also known as weems). A weem was a thatched stone hut, or series of huts, from which ran a stone-slabbed underground tunnel, sometimes sixty-five yards long, with a drain running under the floor. There are remains of a number of these curiosities in various parts of Scotland, including three around Dundee.

Unique to Scotland, where some of them still brood over the landscape, are the brochs, first built about 100 B.C. and inhabited for about six hundred years. Remains of some five hundred brochs have been found, most of them close to the coast and to good farming land. These towering, circular structures, each as high as a four-storey block of flats, and about forty-five feet across, were built entirely of roughly-shaped stone blocks, with no cement or mortar to bind them together. There were no openings on the outside, except a single, tiny entrance, leading into an easily-defended tunnel. For extra security, broch people lived entirely within the walls of their strongholds, in rooms and galleries on several levels. A broch was a burglar-proof safe, big enough to house several families and their animals in time of danger. As most brochs are on the north and northeast coasts, and in Orkney and the Western Isles, it is reasonable to assume that a sea-attack was expected at one time from across the North Sea. As to who these potential invaders were, history is silent. And, of course, when the invasion did come, in A.D. 80, it was from the south, and on foot.

To the Romans, Caledonia, as they called the lands north of the Firth of Forth, with its inhospitable terrain, appalling climate, and elusive people, must have seemed like the end of the world. Indeed it was the end of the Roman world, for it was the farthest north that the legions penetrated, and it was never conquered. Commanded by Agricola, one of Rome's most brilliant generals, and most humane governors, they came in two great columns, one up the west coast of Britain and the other to the east. The tribes below the Forth capitulated. They had not learned to fight as a single force.

The northern tribes were a different proposition altogether, though we know practically nothing about them, apart from the name of their leader, Calgacus the Swordsman. It is believed that some of them painted or tattooed their torsos, which they displayed in battle, and that others wore trousers and gaily coloured shirts. And a Roman writer comments on a people on the Continent of a similar background to the Caledonians: 'The men let their moustaches grow so long that their mouths are covered up;

and so, when they eat, these get entangled in their food, while their drink is taken in, as it were, through a strainer.' Agricola had to settle for a long campaign. He sited forts – there was a notable one at Inchtuthil in Perthshire, and he sent contingents of marines along the east coast by ship, to soften up the natives. Finally, in 84, he brought Calgacus and the tribes to battle at Mons Graupius, which may have been the mountain now called Bennachie, and soundly defeated them.

That was not the end of Caledonian resistance, by any means. In 122, the Emperor Hadrian, on a personal reconnaissance, decided to stop worrying about them and to make the wall, which he was building from the Tyne to the Solway, the northern boundary of the province of Britain. In about 140, however, in the reign of Antoninus, the boundary was once more extended, to a new wall across the isthmus between the Firths of Clyde and Forth. Made of turf, with a wooden rampart on top, it had sixteen forts along its thirty-eight miles. In 155, the tribes broke through, and knocked it down. The Romans forced them back, and rebuilt the wall. Then, in about 180, they took up their belongings, destroyed their forts, and retreated beyond Hadrian's Wall for good.

When the Romans abandoned Britain altogether, in about 410, the northern part was inhabited by four distinct peoples – the Picts, the Scots, the Britons, and the Angles. The Picts are first heard of at the end of the third century A.D. Their name comes from the Latin *picti*, meaning 'painted ones'. They were a warlike race of Celtic origin, who originally established a kingdom covering all the lands north of the Firths of Clyde and Forth. They have left behind some pictures of themselves and weird symbols and representations of animals, all carved in stone. They spoke a form of Celtic, and also an unknown language of their own, which appears as inscriptions, but which no one has managed to decipher. We do, however, have a list of some of their kings, with resounding names like Brude, Gartnait, Domlech, Kenneth, Angus, Foith, and Verb, and from this it appears that succession was through the female line. A king could be succeeded by his brother, that is, by a son of his royal mother, or by his sister's or his daughter's son, but never by his own son.

In 563, Columba came from Ireland to the heathen Picts. He was a high-ranking prince who had given up everything, including his name, to become a monk and a missionary. The story goes that he had once made a copy of an illuminated book of psalms which he had borrowed. The owner of the original book demanded that the copy be handed over as well. Columba refused. Sides were taken, and there was a battle in which many were killed. Columba, appalled at the slaughter he had caused, resolved to leave his country and to convert to Christianity as many heathens as the number of men who had died as a result of the dispute – the first recorded copyright controversy. Columba was politely, rather than enthusiastically, received by the Pictish king, who did, however, offer him the miniscule island of Iona on which to build a monastery. From Iona, Columba's disciples went out, founding other monasteries and building churches.

In a remarkably short time, by about 620, most Picts had become Christians, and the great, decorative standing stones, which are today the most tangible reminder of that people, began to be carved in the form of crosses.

St Columba was by no means the first Irishman to make a home in Pictish territory. In the fourth century A.D., a fierce people, the Dal Riata, crossed the water and settled in the west, where Argyll is now. They were known as 'Scotti', or Scots, which probably means 'pirates' or 'raiders', and that is what they seem to have been. Together with the Picts, the Scots harried the Romans, and when the Romans had left Britain, they harried the Picts instead, to such effect that in about 500, the Dal Riata, under Fergus, had made Argyll their permanent home, and established there the capital of a kingdom. Firm royal succession was ensured by a system whereby the eldest, or most able, of the king's immediate male relatives was elected, in the king's lifetime, to succeed him. In about 843, it seems that the Picts, weakened by a series of attacks by marauding Vikings from Scandinavia, were heavily defeated by Kenneth MacAlpin, King of the Scots, who now became King of the Picts, too. The new, united, kingdom became known as Scotia, and Kenneth I as the first King of Scotland. Gaelic, the Celtic dialect which the Scots brought with them from Ireland, was soon the language of the whole region.

For an account of the two peoples in the lands below the Firths of Clyde and Forth, we must go back in time again. Originally, this region had been occupied by tribes of Britons, one of whose kingdoms was Strathclyde, 'Valley of the Clyde', in which, in about 543, the time of King Roderick of Strathclyde, Glasgow was founded. When Glasgow had become a flourishing market town, Edinburgh was just a hill fort on a rock. The fort was called Din Eidyn, and was the headquarters of the kingdom of Gododdin. Though Strathclyde continued to be a separate kingdom after King Roderick, Gododdin came to a sticky end.

Much of the region now called the Borders was occupied by a warrior race from Germany, the Angles, who had swept up the east coast of Britain and founded their own kingdom there. Gododdin was now sandwiched between the Picts across the Forth and the Angles in Northumbria. In about 600, the King of Gododdin got together a small army, including a detachment of knights from Wales, and rode out against the Angles' capital at Catterick. They had a long way to go, and when they got there, they fought like demons, but to no avail. Only three of them returned, one of them being the Welsh poet Aneirin, who wrote a poem about this ill-fated expedition.

Now, of course, the Angles swept into the lands of Gododdin, took Din Eidyn, and settled in the region themselves. They remained there until 1018, when Malcolm II raised a mighty army not only from his own kingdom of Scotia, but also of Britons from Strathclyde. He smashed the Angles at Carham, and took back the lands which had once belonged to Gododdin. And when, that same year, the King of Strathclyde died, Malcolm took that kingdom for Scotia, too. Now the country of Scotland was complete, and as it has been ever since. The Angles' legacy to the Scottish nation, however, was a significant one. While the Highlanders retained their Gaelic, which is still used today by twenty per cent of the population of the Highlands, Lowlanders came to speak a form of English brought by the Angles. Now, English is spoken all over Scotland.

Two other distinct people of the past contributed their customs, culture, names and genes to the Scottish race. For hundreds of years, the inhabitants of Scotia used to pray to be delivered from 'the fury of the Vikings', but many were not. The Vikings did not even spare the holy island of Iona, and one ghastly day in 825 they massacred the entire community. Not all Vikings, however, came to kill and loot. Many arrived in their longships as immigrants, because there was no room and no food for them at home. They settled especially in Orkney and Shetland, in the Hebrides and on the west coast. They brought their own customs and art, and their own way of burying the dead, putting into the grave, alongside the body, valuable things for the spirit's journey. These Scottish Vikings were farmers and fishermen. Orkney and Shetland remained Viking territory until 1468, when they were handed back to Scotland as part of the dowry of the King of Norway's daughter, on her marriage to James III. In fact, they were only lent, until Norway could raise the full sum in cash. They have never been redeemed. Today, Orcadians and Shetlanders celebrate their Viking origins in their place-names; by calling their daughters Ingrid or Thora, for instance, and their sons Eric or Magnus; and by retaining some of the ancient customs and festivals, of which Up-Helly-A, in January, is the most spectacular.

The Normans came to Scotland not as conquerors, as they had to England, but at the invitation of David I, to help him govern the country. They introduced the feudal system, and established burghs as centres for trade and as markets. Their influence was profound on the royal succession of Scotland, and then of England, too, which stretches in a virtually unbroken line from Kenneth MacAlpin to Elizabeth (II of England). The great-grandfather of Robert the Bruce was a Norman. Robert's daughter Marjorie married Walter, hereditary Steward, or Stewart, of Scotland, a title conferred on his Norman ancestor by David I. And from Walter and Marjorie descended the line of Stewart monarchs who reigned for almost three hundred and fifty years.

The Irish influence did not, of course, end with the Dal Riata. Between 1800 and 1850, and especially at times of famine when the potato crops failed, hundreds of thousands of Irish men and women came to Scotland to seek work, and many of them settled in Glasgow. The fare from Belfast was about 5d, and the boats that sailed into the Clyde were packed so tight that any who died on the voyage were held upright in the press of bodies until the passengers disembarked. A smaller wave of immigrants began to come in the early part of the nineteenth century, too. They were Jews from Europe, seeking freedom from oppression, a freedom they readily found in Scotland. The first Jewish synagogue in Scotland was founded in Edinburgh in 1821. Among the members of the congregation were a 'dentist and corn-operator'; an 'umbrella and leather cap maker'; a 'patent medicine vendor'; a 'spectacle maker'; a 'sealing wax manufacturer'; a 'quill merchant'; a 'black lead and pencil manufacturer'; a 'straw hat maker'; and Philip Levy, 'Furrier to His Majesty', who in 1860 was granted Royal Letters Patent 'for his new Invention of Fur Sac or Wrapper whereby the feet as well as the knees are constantly kept warm and comfortable'.

If you go into a school today, particularly in or around Glasgow, among the children with first names or surnames of Irish, Pictish, Viking, British, English, Norman and Jewish origin, you will find those who have names from India, Pakistan, Iran, Hong Kong, Malaysia, and other countries of the East. There is an Islamic centre on the south bank of the Clyde, and mosques in other cities, most of which contain Sikh and Buddhist communities, too. Both Glasgow and Edinburgh have Hindu temples. The distinctions between the peoples who forged the Scottish race are being further blurred, but the distinction in being Scottish remains.

Kings and Queens

Kenneth MacAlpin was proclaimed King of the Picts and Scots on the ancient Stone of Destiny, an irregular block of stone said to have been the pillow on which Jacob was resting when he had the miraculous dream at Bethel, and brought by the Scots from Ireland. Kenneth made Scone in Perthshire his chief town and here, on Moot Hill, he installed the Stone. Though he transferred the holy relics of St Columba from Iona to a new church at Dunkeld, he maintained the Pictish royal tradition, which lasted for another two hundred years after him, of being buried in Iona. At a time when an expected life-span was short, and that of a king even shorter, he died of a tumour after ruling for sixteen years, and was succeeded, according to the custom of the Scots, by his brother Donald.

From the accession of Donald I in 859 to that of Malcolm II in 1005, there were fourteen Kings of Scotia. Of the ten whose manner of death is recorded, nine were killed in battle or murdered by rivals. The longest serving of them, Constantine II, abdicated after forty-three years, perhaps under pressure from relations who felt that after all that time another branch of the family ought to have the chance to be king. Malcom II, the first King of Scotland as we know it, was also the last of the line of Alpin. He had killed his two predecessors in a bloody passage to the throne, and broken with Scottish tradition by ensuring that he was succeeded by Duncan I, his grandson by a daughter, thus also providing William Shakespeare with the basis of the tragedy of *Macbeth*. 'The gracious Duncan', however, was neither particularly gracious nor the greybeard that Shakespeare depicts. He was not yet forty when he was killed in battle against his cousin Macbeth, who, under Scottish law, had just as much right to be king as Duncan. Macbeth ruled firmly but not ungenerously for seventeen years, and found time to go on a pilgrimage to Rome, where he scattered money to the poor. He was finally defeated by Duncan's son, Malcolm – a cairn marks the spot at Lumphanan, west of Aberdeen, where his body was said to have been buried before being taken to Iona. Even so, Malcolm still had to dispose of Lulach, Macbeth's stepson, who had been elected king under Scottish law.

Malcolm III (known as 'Canmore', or 'Big-headed') was a bluff, warrior-type, who spoke Gaelic, English, and Latin, but apparently never got round to being able to read or write any of them. In an attempt to extend his kingdom, he invaded England, killing innocent civilians or bringing them back with him as slaves. The English king, William the Conqueror, came north, forced Malcolm to submit, and took his eldest son, Duncan, back with him as hostage. Malcolm took no notice and made two more sorties. After William's death in 1087, Duncan was returned. Malcolm then perpetrated a further act of aggression against England, but was ambushed and killed on his way home. In spite of his boorish ways, he made two diplomatic marriages: first to the widow of the troublesome Earl of Orkney and Caithness, and then to the saintly Margaret, a princess of the old English line. Margaret had a Christianising influence on Scotland and a civilising effect on Malcolm, and the rude fort on the rock of Edinburgh became a royal castle, enclosing the tiny chapel which bears her name.

There was an attempt by Donald III (Shakespeare's Donalbain and brother of Malcolm) to restore the Scottish way of succession – he actually ruled twice, briefly – but from the accession in 1097 of Edgar, eldest son of Malcolm and Margaret, the throne devolved by inheritance. In 1249, the youngest king yet, Alexander III, seven years old, succeeded his father, who had died, unusually for a monarch, on board ship, while trying to wrest the Hebrides from Norway. He was married, at ten, to Margaret, daughter of Henry III, which ensured peace between Scotland and England for a time. In 1263, after preventing, at the Battle of Largs, a Viking invasion, Alexander made peace and, as a token of its permanence, married his daughter Margaret to the King of Norway in 1281. Alexander's reign represented the longest golden age of peace and prosperity that Scotland ever had as an independent nation. His family life, however, was fraught with tragedy. His wife died in 1275, and then his two sons succumbed, followed by his daughter in 1283. The heir to the throne of Scotland was now Margaret's infant daughter, another Margaret, the 'Maid of Norway'. Desperate for a son, Alexander married Yolande de Dreux, a Frenchwoman. Five months later, he was returning to her one stormy night after a meeting in Edinburgh, when his horse missed its footing. The next morning his body was found on the shore below.

A committee of two earls, two bishops and two barons, known as the Guardians, was formed to run the country. True to dynastic principles, they invited the Maid of Norway to return as queen, but she died on the voyage. With thirteen men now claiming the throne, the Guardians asked the advice of Edward I of England, who adjudicated in favour of John Balliol, the senior surviving relative of Alexander III. He was also a weak man, which suited Edward, and in 1296 he was deposed. Scotland now had no king, and the English surged all over the land. For a time, William Wallace led the Scottish resistance movement, but in 1295 he was betrayed, taken to London, and executed in disgusting fashion. Robert the Bruce, a distant but direct descendant of David I, stabbed his nearest rival, John Comyn, in an argument and later had himself crowned Robert I at Scone, though not on the Stone of Destiny. That symbol of Scottish independence had been removed to London by Edward I. It took Robert eight years to get rid of the English, which he did gloriously at the battle of Bannockburn in 1314, but it was only after fourteen more years of Scottish invasion tactics that Edward III signed a treaty acknowledging Scotland's independence once again.

Robert's son, David II, died without children. The heir was Robert II, son of the Bruce's daughter Marjorie and Walter the Steward (or Stewart), the sixth to hold that hereditary title. Stewart monarchs ruled Scotland for 343 years, and, for 111 of those, England, too, but at this time the two countries were still enemies. The 'Auld Alliance', forged by Robert I, was with France, which, like Scotland, had reason to regret English invasions. In 1406, the elderly Robert III, fearing for the safety of his surviving son, twelve-year-old James, in a country where administration was chaotic, sent him to France by ship. James never arrived. He was kidnapped by the English. Now King of Scotland – his father had died on hearing the news – he was made to stay in England until he was thirty. Then he was sent home to be crowned, with a bill of £40,000 for his board and lodging. James was a man in a hurry. An administrator with a grim sense of humour, as well as a poet and a sportsman, he executed his opponents, cleared up the confusion, and re-established the efficacy of Parliament. Then he was stabbed to death while taking a Christmas break in a monastery in Perth.

James II grew up to rid himself of two trouble-making families, the Douglases and the Livingstones, but was then himself despatched by an exploding cannon. His son, James III, also ran into problems with his nobles, and was finally murdered while escaping from the battlefield where they had produced his fifteen-year old son as their leader. James IV lived long enough to reform the education system, introduce printing, and encourage the arts and science. He set up building programmes, re-equipped his army and navy, and married Margaret Tudor, daughter of Henry VII of England, thus establishing the dynastic link which was later to unite the two crowns. Then he fell victim to the conditions of the Auld Alliance. When Henry VIII invaded France in 1513, James had no option but to attack England. At Flodden, he was challenged to battle. He and the flower of his army and administration were slaughtered.

James V could be generous as well as acquisitive, and kind as well as vengeful. To him is attributed the alias of 'The Good Man of Ballengeich', under which he went about meeting his subjects as one of themselves. He opposed Protestantism, and when Henry VIII made trouble about James's refusal to back him against the Pope, the Scottish King, much against his councillors' advice, sent an invading army into England, with disastrous results. Overcome, it is said, by depression, he retired to Falkland Palace. On being told that his second wife, Mary of Guise, had had a daughter, now heir to the throne after the death the previous year of both his sons, he is supposed to have turned his face to the wall and died, after observing, 'It came with a lass: it will end with a lass', or words to that effect. If he was referring to the royal Stewart line, which 'came' with Robert I's daughter Marjorie, he was remarkably percipient, though the end was some time away.

Mary Stuart (this form of the surname was used by her and her descendants, there being no 'w' in the French alphabet) was less than a week old when she became 'Queen of Scots'. She spent most of her childhood in France, married the heir to the throne and, on the death of Henry II in 1559, became Queen of France. A year later, she was a widow, and in 1561, still only nineteen, she returned to Scotland. Tall, attractive and energetic, she was a sound ruler who allowed her people, in the throes of the Reformation, to worship as they pleased. She was also, however, headstrong, Catholic, and the great-granddaughter of Henry VII, and these innate and inherited factors caused her downfall and her ultimate execution at the hands of Elizabeth I. Mary fell in love with her unsuitable cousin, Lord Darnley, and married him; then became enamoured of the even more unsavoury Earl of Bothwell, whom she was able to marry after the violent death of Darnley in highly suspicious circumstances. Forced to abdicate in favour of her baby son, James, she took refuge in England in 1568, only to be imprisoned for the rest of her life. For many Catholics, and others in England, regarded Elizabeth as illegitimate and thus disbarred from the throne, and Mary herself as their lawful queen.

The baby James VI, son of Mary and Darnley, was carried at his coronation in the arms of the Earl of Mar. His childhood was largely spent as the pawn of one side or the other in the continuous struggle for political supremacy, and his early manhood in financial straits, waiting for Elizabeth to die. When she did, in 1603, he was King of England, too. With his queen and his court he moved to London, and only returned to Scotland once in his life. Awkward in appearance and gait, he had disgusting table manners and he never washed his hands. He was fascinated by witchcraft, about which he wrote a book. His sobriquet, 'The Wisest Fool in Christendom', belied his diplomatic cunning. He left to Scotland, however, years of strife and slaughter, initiated by his insistence that he, and not the Presbyterian General Assembly, was the supreme Head of the Church, which must be governed by bishops appointed by him.

Charles I came to Edinburgh in 1633 for his Scottish coronation. His attempt in 1637 to impose on Scotland the English style of church service led to riots and the mobilisation of the Covenanters, committed to fight for their own religion. In 1640, the Scottish Parliament abolished rule by bishops and removed the King from his position of Head of the Church. When he refused to allow the Presbyterian form of worship in England, the Scots came into the Civil War on the Parliament side. After Charles's final defeat, he asked the Scots for sanctuary. When he still refused to establish Presbyterianism in England, they handed him over to Cromwell's Parliament, little knowing what his fate would be.

Embarrassed at the execution of Charles I, and not liking any better the military interventions of Cromwell, the Scottish Parliament invited Charles's son to come out of exile in Holland, and he was crowned Charles II of Scotland at Scone in 1651. He immediately led the Scottish army into England, was predictably defeated by a larger force, and went back into exile. When he was returned to the English throne in 1660, he repudiated his promise to support the Covenant and appointed bishops to Scotland. This inflamed the Covenanters to violence again, and, after their defeat at Bothwell Brig in 1679 at the hands of Charles's illegitimate son, the Duke of Monmouth, they turned to warfare. A more lasting and pleasing legacy of Charles II is the present Palace of Holyroodhouse, rebuilt to his specifications, though he never set foot in it.

James VII (and II of England), Charles's brother, was Catholic. Even harsher measures were imposed on the Covenanters, and when, in 1687, he granted freedom of worship, this deceived no one. It was clearly the prelude to establishing Catholicism as the national religion in England and Scotland. Protestant William of Orange and his wife Mary, James's daughter, were invited to be joint rulers. James fled to France, to join his wife and infant son, James Edward Stuart. In spite of William's allowing the establishment of the Church of Scotland, many Scots were even more suspicious of him than they had been of James, whose son they regarded as their rightful king. The effects of the Jacobite rebellions, notably those of 1715 and 1745, still reverberate. On William's death, Mary's sister Anne began her glittering reign, memorable also for the Union of the English and Scottish Parliaments in 1709. Though she had seventeen children, she died without an heir, so the royal line of the Stewarts did 'end with a lass', and the succession passed to the descendants of Elizabeth of Bohemia, sister of Charles I, known as the Winter Queen.

When George IV came to Edinburgh in 1822, it was the first visit by a reigning British monarch for over a hundred and fifty years. There was some mirth, and sourness, as well as celebration. The King, a man of considerable girth, had been advised to wear full Highland dress, which annoyed the southern Scottish folk. One official, faced with the presence of a fat man in a kilt, knelt and kissed his hand. It was not the King, but one of his attendants, who were all in kilts, too. 'Wrong, by Jove,' cried the worthy and moved on unabashed to the correct, and even larger, kilted shape.

Faulty stage management also dogged the first visit of Queen Victoria, then aged twenty-three, and Prince Albert in 1842. Because bad weather had delayed the royal yacht, no one was waiting to hand her the keys of Edinburgh when she arrived, so the royal carriage swept through the city and out to Dalkeith, with the councillors, routed from their breakfasts, in vain pursuit. Further visits were better organised, and Victoria's love of the Highlands, and her book, *Leaves from the Journal of our Life in the Highlands*, had much to do with the development of the Scottish tourist industry. Balmoral Castle, rebuilt to her husband's specifications, became a family home, the first in Scotland for the royal family since the time of James VI. Today, it is regularly used for royal holidays, and Holyroodhouse, repaired and refurbished for George V, is a royal palace once more, used once a year by his granddaughter as a state residence. In common with numerous of her predecessors, she was crowned in Westminster Abbey in 1953 on the Stone of Destiny, which was 'acquired' from the Scots by Edward I. It was a near thing, however, for in 1950, a group of Scottish students broke into the Abbey, removed the Stone, and brought it back to Scotland. It was later returned, but the point had been made.

Clan and Tartan

The Normans introduced feudalism to Scotland. This form of social order gave some protection to the common folk who were at the lowest level in the chain of subservience, and depended ultimately on service to the Crown, which had granted the land on which they lived to their lord. In the Gaelic-speaking Highlands, that region to the north and west of the imaginary 'Highland Line', a boundary running northeast from Dumbarton to Ballater and then to Nairn (following the course of the Grampian Moutains), a much older social structure already existed. The tenure of land under the clan system was much the same as under feudalism, for the clan chief owned the clan territory. The land was held communally by the members of the clan, who in return rendered service to their chief. The imposition of feudalism on the clans caused considerable strain when the interests of the chief and the feudal overlord, or the clan and the Crown, were at variance, for the tradition of the clans called for utter obedience to the chief, whose will was law. The feudal lords, and sometimes the king himself, were persistently required to deal with local outbreaks of insubordination, where these occurred within reach. Thus, in the more inaccessible western Highlands, the Lord of the Isles, a title which resided with Clan Donald, ruled like a sovereign.

Clann means 'children', and kinship was at the heart of the system. All members of one clan, or one sept (that is, a clan branch), had the same name, derived from an historical or legendary ancestor, which bound them together. Theoretically they had a blood-relationship with one another, but in practice, often only the chief of the clan and the chieftains of the septs were strictly related. Loyalty and obedience were paramount and unquestioning: any divergence was rigorously punished. There is a story of an unfortunate clansman who incurred the displeasure of Duncan Campbell, seventh Laird of Glenorchy and ancestor of the Campbells of Breadalbane, known as Black Duncan of the Cowl. When faced with the inevitable dangling noose, the man showed some reluctance to approach it. His wife, standing at his side, pushed him forward, with the immortal words, 'Just another step, Colin, to please the laird!'

Members of a clan, or followers of a particular chieftain, wore a plant badge, often not so much as a means of identification as a talisman. The MacDonalds sported various species of heather, the Campbells gale or bog myrtle. The badge of the Grants is Scots pine. Mistletoe is the sign of the Hays, and fern that of the Chisolms. Bonnie Prince Charlie, son of James Edward Stuart, wore the thistle and the white rose of the Royal House of Stewart during the Jacobite rebellion of 1745. George IV, in his incongruous effort to prove his Scottish ancestry (which was genuine) wore the thistle in his bonnet when he landed at Leith in 1822 though, of course, he was not a Stuart.

What is regarded as 'Highland dress' is of comparatively recent development, though its origins are old enough and, like many cultural traditions, are based on practical sense. When homes were rudimentary and cold, and damp clothes spelt chills and other illnesses, bare legs were the answer for both men and women moving about the wet, marshy and often treacherous terrain. A sixteenth-century Scottish history refers to Highlanders wearing, under a shaggy rug used as a cloak, a shirt that reached the knees with, for decency, some kind of underpants. The traditional view that a Highlander wears nothing beneath his kilt has, therefore, been dying hard ever since, though an eyewitness records that Bonnie Prince Charlie, in his nightmare escapes through bogs, burns and mudholes after the battle of Culloden in 1746, was certainly in just such a state of underdress.

In the 1600s men began to wrap their plaids round their bodies. The plaid was a vast blanket of tartan (that is, patterned with stripes), five feet wide and sixteen feet long, close-woven and midge proof. For travellers out in the open on the hills and moors in winter, it served both as a covering and a tent. To put it on, you set it on the ground lengthwise and laid down on it, gathering the stuff around you and securing it with a belt. When you stood up, the bottom half formed a pleated skirt. You then draped the top half over your shoulders and across your chest. The plaid was such a basic part of a Highlander's dress that when the men on the left wing of the Earl of Mar's army at the battle of the Sheriffmuir in 1715 lost their plaids, they had to go home and reclothe themselves. Many did not return.

Working in a blanket was unwieldy, and in the early 1700s the habit developed of cutting the plaid in half and attaching one piece to the waistband. Thus was the kilt invented. The brogue, today a leather shoe with decorative holes scored in the upper, was originally an essentially practical form of footwear for use on wet ground. It comprised a thin leather sole, and an upper punched with holes to let the water out.

The raw wool from which plaids were woven was first stood in human urine, then washed and dried, before being spun and then boiled in vegetable dyes. Though people from a particular region or clan may have tended to wear the same basic colour so that their homeland could be recognised when travelling, clan tartans were not invented until the eighteenth century. After the failure of the Jacobite rebellion in 1746, every form of Highland dress was proscribed by law, in an effort to bring the social structure of the northern clans in line with that of the southern parts of Scotland. Even clans like the Campbells and the MacDonalds of Skye, who had fought for the Government side, were affected by the ban. The only exceptions were the Highland regiments serving abroad, whose uniforms were based on that of the Black Watch, formed in 1739. When the ban was lifted in 1782, the skills and traditions associated with weaving and wearing the tartan had largely been forgotten. Their revival, initially as a luxury and a pastime for the better-off, came in the nineteenth century, fostered by the publication of a bogus ancient manuscript describing thirty-eight specific family tartans and patterns. The elaborate classification of clan tartans, and today's Highland dress – the *philabeg* (little kilt), sporran, tweed jacket and waistcoat, brogues, and woollen stockings (into the right one of which is stuck the ceremonial dagger, the *sgian dubh*) – stem from that time, too.

At times of danger, especially when inter-clan warfare threatened, selected clansmen went out, carrying the fiery cross. One side of its horizontal piece was ablaze (or at least charred); the other had attached to it a bloodstained cloth. At this sign, all male members of the clan gathered at an appointed meeting ground.

Within the clan, a rough code of honour would be scrupulously observed. In times when warfare was a natural way of life, however, and another clan's property, especially cattle, was regarded as fair game when one was short oneself, inter-clan hostilities and vendettas were so commonplace and energetically indulged in that some lasted for generations. A comparatively civilised, if that is the word, encounter took place between two clans, said to be the Davidsons and the Macphersons, or between two septs of those names within Clan Chattan, at the North Inch of Perth in 1396. The original cause of the dispute was common enough. Some years before, Clan Chattan had fought the Camerons. The Macphersons and the Davidsons each claimed the honour of going into battle on Chattan's right wing. The altercation developed into a feud, and the feud into the confrontation at the North Inch, at which thirty chosen champions battled it out for each side. The result is obscure, but it is known that there were few survivors. A similar, but more spectacular, match was played some years later between the Mackays and the Murrays, six hundred on each side, from which only nine men came out alive when time was called.

The most legendary clansman of them all, Rob Roy MacGregor, belonged to the most notorious clan, though history suggests that the MacGregors were sinned against as much as they sinned themselves. It was largely the rough and often brutal expansionist policies of the Campbells and the subsequent retaliation by the MacGregors that led to the latter being officially declared *personae non gratae* in the reign of Mary, Queen of Scots. Matters got further out of hand some years later after what was, for those days, a minor incident. Two MacGregors, on their way home from Glasgow, called at a Colquhoun house and asked for hospitality, as they were entitled to do. When they were refused, they settled themselves for the night in a barn and, being hungry, killed a sheep, part of which they ate. The next morning they were apprehended and, though they offered to pay for the sheep, were summarily hanged. The MacGregors retaliated against this breach of good manners by despatching a raiding party into Colquhoun land, which killed two Colquhouns and lifted nine hundred head of cattle and sundry other domestic animals. The Colquhouns responded with a deplorable piece of stage-management.

They paraded in front of James VI at Stirling a whole bevy of spurious 'widows' of the attack, mounted on horseback, each bearing on the point of a spear a bloody shirt, which had for the purpose of the exhibition been dipped in sheep's blood. James, who, apparently, could not stand the sight of blood in any form, immediately renewed the orders allowing the MacGregors to be persecuted.

The MacGregors, egged on by the chief of the Campbells, who had everything to gain from the feud, got together a force of three hundred men and set out for Colquhoun territory. The Colquhouns were waiting for them with five hundred foot and three hundred cavalry, but were routed and lost in addition six hundred more of their cattle. (For good measure, the MacGregors also slaughtered a number of innocent citizens of Dumbarton, who had simply come out to watch the spectacle.) James took all this as a personal affront and, on the very day in 1603 that he left Edinburgh to secure the other half of his kingdom, he approved an Act of Council not only outlawing the MacGregors, but even abolishing their name.

The chief of the MacGregors was caught and executed: eighteen of his leading clansmen were hanged, drawn and quartered, and their lands were confiscated. There was, however, sympathy for the clan in the Highlands, and many were the people who befriended and sheltered its scattered remnants, in spite of the harsh penalties for doing so. One Rory Mackenzie, owner of the estate of Kintail, was fined £4,000 (Scots), the equivalent of about £60,000 in today's money! It was due to men like him that the clan was able to survive, though it was not until 1774 that the ban was finally, and formally, lifted.

Rob Roy MacGregor was the third son of a minor chieftain. He differs from Robin Hood in that he certainly existed, and many of the legendary exploits attributed to him are true. As was usual in those times, he followed the Highland trade of cattle-rustler as well as drover, supplementing his income by an ingenious variation on the practice of insurance, known even in those times as 'blackmail'. He offered to protect the herds of wealthy landowners in return for payment. If the payment was refused, he and his men took the cattle instead. His 'heroic' period was sparked off in 1712 when his chief assistant disappeared with a large sum of money entrusted to Rob by the Duke of Montrose to buy cattle. When Rob could not repay the debt in one instalment, Montrose declared him an outlaw, turned his wife and children out of their home, and destroyed it. Rob retaliated by collecting the Montrose rents at gun-point, and even kidnapped the rent-collector, whom he released when the Duke refused to pay the ransom. After the rebellion of 1715 – Rob fought on the Jacobite side at Sheriffmuir – he was sought also by the Government. Twice he was actually captured, but escaped. He was never caught again, and died quietly in his home at the advanced age of sixty-three.

Another people whom the Campbells persistently harried was Clan Macdonald, and appropriately enough it was the Macdonalds who, in 1645, delivered the coup de grâce to the Campbells as a major fighting force. The Campbell chief, the Marquis of Argyll, supported the Covenanters. His personal enemy, the Marquis of Montrose, was ranging the Highlands with his army, bent on keeping Charles I on his throne. It was December, and Argyll had retired to the comparative comfort and safety of his castle at Inveraray. Montrose found a way through the mountains and attacked. Argyll managed to get away in a boat, but his fighting men were all killed. The rest of the Campbells, three thousand men-at-arms, now went after Montrose's exhausted force of fifteen hundred. Montrose, by one of the most astonishing exploits in British warfare, outflanked them in a forced march over mountain passes blocked by snow and ice. He came up behind them at Inverlochy with an army which had had virtually nothing to eat for two days. The Macdonalds were in the second line of attack. Montrose lost four men: the opposition, largely due to the vengefulness of the Macdonalds, fifteen hundred.

The collapse of the clan system in the latter half of the eighteenth century began with the deliberate policy of the Government to prevent any further rebellions, though the Highlander now became, for the first time, a free man, answerable only to the Crown in matters of justice, and under no obligation to take up arms at the will of his chief. The chiefs, stripped of their responsibility as well as their authority, and having, in the case of many of them, expended their capital to support Bonnie Prince Charlie, had little alternative but trade. So when influential and rich sheep farmers from the south made offers for land which was simply not viable for crofting, these were hard to refuse. The notorious Highland Clearances depopulated the land, caused enforced emigration, and effectively destroyed the kinship of the clan. There emerged, however, something which may prove as lasting – the fellowship of clan, engendered by the dispersal of Highland Scots throughout the world, reinforced by the foundation of clan societies, and fostered by the ease and comparative comfort of modern air travel.

The Highlands

There is an unusual but historical link between the first Highland king to be recorded as wearing a kilt and the last King of Scotland to be buried in the island of Iona. Shortly after the death and the burial in Iona of Donald III in 1097, his successor, Edgar, made a treaty with Magnus 'Barelegs', King of Norway, acknowledging Norwegian sovereignty over all the islands off the west coast – Magnus's attempt to have Kintyre classified as an island by having himself dragged in a ship across the isthmus at Tarbert was, very properly, regarded as sharp practice. Even so, there were Norse incursions and forceful acquisitions on the mainland until well into the twelfth century, when they were finally stopped by the powerful Lord of Argyll, Somerled. He himself was killed in 1164, leading an invasion of southwest Scotland, and his enormous dominions, which he had obtained by inheritance and by two very advantageous marriages, were divided among his four sons – these included the island groups centred on Mull and Islay, which he held as a vassal of Norway. From the eldest son, Dougall, are descended the Macdougalls. Norse control of

the western isles was ended in spectacular fashion by Alexander III in 1263 when, at the Battle of Largs, he not only successfully defended the mainland against a huge Norwegian fleet commanded by King Haakon, but sent it packing.

Highlanders were prominent in the War of Independence against England, but among those especially loyal to Robert the Bruce in the dark days immediately following the murder of Comyn was Angus Og of Islay, who was to lead the men of the Isles at Bannockburn, after which his grateful king rewarded him with Mull as well. Angus's son, John Macdonald of Islay, from whom almost all Macdonalds claim descent, acquired, through two marriages and by gift of David II, the Outer Hebrides and Kintyre and, in 1354, proudly assumed the official title of 'Lord of the Isles'. The package seemed to be complete when the second Lord acquired, through marriage, the earldom of Ross, as well as the island of Skye. The snag was that the Duke of Albany, Regent of Scotland for James I, who was still unavoidably detained in England by Henry IV, wanted Ross for *his* son. In 1411, Donald, Lord of the Isles, gathered at Inverness a force of ten thousand Highlanders and men of the Isles, and swept towards Aberdeen, which in effect meant that he was invading the Lowlands. The Regent's army met him at Harlaw, where a finely and gallantly contested battle ended in a draw.

James I, when he finally obtained his release from England in 1424, had to decide quickly what to do about the potentially disruptive influence of the Highland chiefs. He restored Ross to Alexander, the new Lord of the Isles, who promptly made further trouble. James, who was a master tactician, invited Alexander and some forty other chiefs to a Parliament at Inverness, which they dutifully and gullibly attended. As each man entered the hall, he was seized and thrown into jail, while James amused himself, and the rest of the company, by making up and reciting Latin verses. The less important prisoners were hanged, beheaded, or banished. Alexander was treated to a royal and comfortable period of detention but, having failed to get the message, got together an army on his release, did serious damage to all the Crown lands within reach, and burned Inverness, which was a royal burgh. James's successful counter-attack came as such a surprise to the young Alexander that he had no alternative but to surrender. He was shut up in Tantallon Castle, and then brought to the Abbey of Holyroodhouse to make a public apology. Even so, he only obtained a pardon on the intervention of the Queen.

That was by no means the end of this extended saga of disloyalty. In 1462, in the reign of James III, John, Lord of the Isles, entered into a dastardly agreement with the Earl of Douglas and the English King Edward IV to conquer the whole of Scotland and divide it up between them. The coup failed, and John was deprived of Ross and had his status reduced to that of a mere feudal baron. This did not prevent either his opening further negotiations with England on the accession to the Scottish throne of the young James IV, or his troops from invading the mainland in an effort to win back Ross for their clan chief. The Crown had now had enough.

In 1493, James declared the title of Lord of the Isles defunct and the whole of the territory forfeit. John surrendered a year later, and ended his days in a monastery.

The liquidation of the title and powers of the Lord of the Isles did little, however, to reduce the nuisance value of the territory's chiefs, who enthusiastically resisted the occasional sorties of the royal navy into their waters. And, whereas in the Highlands at large, lawlessness and bloodthirstiness on the part of the nobility were no more rife than they were in the Lowlands, the scale on which they tended to be exercised could not be ignored. As a counter, James VI's Parliament introduced in 1597 an ingenious Act requiring all chiefs and landlords in the Highlands and Isles to produce the title deeds to their property. Where these had been lost, or never existed, the lands were confiscated and handed over to new landlords, whose activities often turned out to be just as destructive to the general welfare of the country. A more successful, and ultimately less drastic, subterfuge was employed by the Bishop of the Isles in 1608. He invited the chiefs in his diocese on board ship to hear a sermon, then kidnapped them. They were released the following year, having agreed to support the Reformed Church, to undertake a measure of disarmament, to eliminate local feuding, to hand over offenders to justice, to send their eldest sons to school in the Lowlands (where, of course, they would be taught in English), and to dispense with the services of their Gaelic bards.

As the influence of the Isles dwindled, that of three clans in particular on the mainland was growing – Gordon in the northeast, Campbell in the southwest, and Mackenzie in the north. When the call came to fight with the Marquis of Montrose for Charles I against the Covenant, the Gordons were for him, the Campbells against, and the Mackenzies wavered. Admittedly, the issues were not clear-cut. Montrose, a young, dashing soldier-poet, had originally subscribed to the Covenant, but changed his allegiance when he foresaw the Scottish Church and Parliament being in the hands of those who would destroy people's freedom. And a Royalist rising in Scotland was seen by Charles and his advisers as an excellent device to entice back home the Scottish forces in England which were fighting for Parliament against him. The predicament of the Earl of Seaforth, clan chief of the Mackenzies, was how to reconcile the Covenant, which he had helped to organise, with his duty to his king. Having failed to do so, he ended his life, as did other Scottish vacillators of noble rank, a Royalist in exile. Montrose's brilliant campaign began in September 1644 with resounding victories against better-equipped and more numerous armies at Tippermuir, Aberdeen (which he afterwards unwisely sacked), Fyvie, Auldearn and Alford, in addition to the fright he gave the Marquis of Argyll and the destruction of the Campbells at Inverlochy. The summer of 1645 saw him heading west towards Glasgow along the foothills below the Ochils, ravaging Campbell property as he went. The Covenanters regrouped and caught up with him at Kilsyth with over six thousand men, only a few hundred of whom survived the ten-minute battle. Montrose was now in Glasgow itself, whose citizens offered £500 if he would stop his Highlanders plundering the city. He accepted. Miffed at being deprived of what they regarded as their lawful subsistence, many of his men returned to their Highland fastnesses.

The defeat of Charles I at Naseby at last released the Scottish troops in England, an army of six thousand. Montrose had only six hundred now, and in spite of acts of great personal gallantry, he was defeated at Philiphaugh, and was reluctantly persuaded to escape to Europe. He returned briefly to the Highlands in 1650, raised only a few men for Charles II, was beaten at Carbisdale, betrayed by Neil Macleod of Assynt, with whom he had sought refuge, and taken south in humiliating fashion, tied to a broken-down horse. It is said that at Pitcaple Castle, one of the night-stops on the way, the wife of the owner showed him a secret way of escape. He refused to take it, preferring to meet his fortune, or fate, in Edinburgh at the hands of his enemies. Though the death sentence had already been passed, the trial still took place. He died with remarkable dignity. Three hours later, his body was removed from the gallows and hacked to pieces. His head was stuck on a spike on the Tolbooth roof (where it is said to have remained until taken down eleven years later to make room for that of the Marquis of Argyll), and the limbs were distributed among the main towns of the land.

Royalist standards were again raised in the Highlands in 1689, when John Graham of Claverhouse, Viscount Dundee, rode out as his cousin Montrose had done, to raise an army against the Government for the exiled James VII. He tamed the more erratic tactics of the Highlanders, and trained them into a disciplined force which shattered the Government army at Killiecrankie. The effort was in vain. A stray bullet caught him at the moment of victory as he encouraged his men. Deprived of their leader, Dundee's army dispersed, but the cause for which they were nominally fighting simmered on. Though King William at last allowed the establishment of the Church of Scotland, governed by its General Assembly, there were many Highlanders (particularly those of Catholic or Episcopalian leanings) who remained faithful to James VII. Their resolve was reinforced when William required all chiefs to sign an oath of allegiance, and further hardened by the outcome of this. Many of them sought, and obtained, James's dispensation for them to sign, which all but two did before the appointed date. MacDonnell of Glengarry was regarded as too powerful to do anything about, but it was decided to make an example of MacIan of Glencoe, Chieftain of a sept of Clan MacDonald. Though he had fully intended to take the oath, he missed the deadline because he went to the wrong place and was then delayed by heavy snow. The subsequent Massacre of Glencoe, on 13 February 1692, though it left only about thirty dead, has gone down in history because of the infamous way in which it was devised and executed.

That Highlanders effectively provided all the armed support for the Jacobite risings of 1715 and 1745 is not to suggest that there were no Jacobites in the Lowlands or even in England. It is simply that Highlanders, with the clan tradition behind them, were looking for a leader, preferably a royal one, and the rest preferred the *status quo* and Protestantism. Ironically, the 1715 rebellion failed through poor leadership. James Edward Stuart, who would have been James VIII, did not turn up in Scotland until all chances of victory had disappeared. The Earl of Mar, known as Bobbing John, probably because of a disability which made him bob up and down as he walked, took the initiative in the campaign because he felt that the interests of Scotland had not been sufficiently taken care of in the Act of Union of 1707, by which the two parliaments were combined and power passed to Westminster. His conduct of the Battle of Sheriffmuir turned a certain victory into a humiliating draw.

Charles Edward Stuart, Bonnie Prince Charlie, did not make the same mistake as his father. He arrived in August 1745, however, in disguise, unannounced, and with just seven companions, claiming the thrones of Scotland and England for James VIII. By force of personality, he rallied many of the clans to him, and by good tactics and a modicum of luck had by the end of September become master of Scotland, and was ready to embark on the more perilous part of his enterprise, the invasion of England. Had he done so at once, instead of staying in Edinburgh to savour his triumph, he might have succeeded. As it was, the few weeks' delay gave the Government time to fetch troops back from the Continent, and to rally thirty thousand professionals against the Prince's five thousand irregular Highlanders. In England, only three hundred recruits joined the Jacobite cause, not even enough to replace the defectors. At Derby, the Prince was advised to turn back. He had a victory at Falkirk, but the writing was on the wall. At Culloden, he was outnumbered, outflanked, and outwitted by the troops under George II's son, the Duke of Cumberland, which included three battalions of Lowland Scots, a Highland battalion, and four companies of Campbells of the Argyll militia. In fact, more Scots fought against Bonnie Prince Charlie than for him during the course of his campaign, and for none was the situation more poignant than for Clan Chisholm, the younger son of whose chief led them at Culloden, while his two elder brothers fought on the Government side as officers in the 21st Regiment.

The rebellion was over, but the legend was only just beginning. For five months the Prince was hunted through Lewis and Skye, and North and South Uist, as well as on the mainland. That he finally escaped to France was due to his good sense and optimistic disposition, and to the bravery and loyalty of those who sheltered and guided him. A reward of £30,000 was offered for his capture. No one ever claimed it. His end, though, was sadly unromantic. Fat, drunken and bloated, he wandered around Europe, and finally died in the arms of his daughter by his long-standing mistress, Clementina Walkinshaw.

During the early part of the eighteenth century, the Highlands had become more accessible through the activities of General Wade who, realising that no professional army could operate there without proper lines of communication, built 243 miles of roads and fifty bridges. The transformation was completed by Thomas Telford who, between 1802 and 1820, built a further twelve hundred bridges and 920 miles of new roads, employing three thousand Highlanders a year in the process. In other respects the employment situation was chaotic, resulting in large scale resettlement and emigration, and general hardship, which was increased by the failure of the potato crop in 1846 and 1848, and again in 1882. The influx of new, and often absentee, landlords from England changed the face of whole tracts of the region, but not the situation – deer forests require even fewer people to run them than sheep farms. Only recently has the tide of opportunity begun to turn. When the North of Scotland Hydro-Electric Board was established in 1943, only one farm in six and one croft in a hundred had electricity. Within twenty years it had built and was administering huge schemes over an area corresponding to two-thirds of the whole of Scotland, including the islands. Today, lines of pylons march across the barren countryside like files of monstrous soldiers. The Highlands and Islands Development Board (1965) encourages local industry and crafts as well as tourism. The hope for the Highlands inspired by the discovery of North Sea oil and gas seems largely extinguished now, but it may flare again.

Magic and Mystery

Belief in the supernatural flourishes particularly in northern lands with marked geographical and natural phenomena, especially rocks, dark lakes, streams and impenetrable forests, and where winter nights are long and Christianity has been inextricably mixed with older, mysterious rites and practices. Scotland is exactly such a land, and the winter nights were the seed-beds in which the stories and incantations, told around the fireside, thrived and were perpetuated.

The early church was realistic. Understanding that many of the old beliefs were too firmly rooted in people's minds to be easily obliterated, it absorbed and adapted them into a Christian pattern. The stone crosses of the Celtic Church often bear pagan symbols, as did some of the Mercat Crosses, which stood in a central position in every burgh and city. This dual tradition is seen in the ancient Gaelic rune of hospitality:

> I saw a stranger yestreen;
> I put food in the eating place,
> Drink in the drinking place,
> Music in the listening place;
> In the sacred name of the Triune;
> He blessed myself and my home,
> My cattle and my dear ones;
> And the lark said in her song,
>   Often, often, often
> Goes the Christ in the stranger's guise,
>   Often, often, often
> Goes the Christ in the stranger's guise.

It is also in the verse to be said when pulling juniper (mountain yew) as a protection on sea and land, and against one's house catching fire:

I will pull the bounteous yew
Through the five bent ribs of Christ,
In the name of the Father, Son, and Holy Ghost,
Against drowning, danger, and confusion.

And in the charm against rheumatism:

Close God about thee,
Look people over thee,
To Christ, or else –
Lift from us the gallows,
Away, away,
Thy poison in the ground,
And thy pain in the stone.

Magical properties were attributed to many other plants: oak, rowan (especially in conjunction with a thread of red silk or wool), elder, yarrow, pearlwort (sometimes used as a love charm), woodbine, St John's wort, bog violet, bramble, figwort, club moss, and mistletoe. A magic hoop of milkwort, butterwort, dandelion and marigold, bound by a triple cord of lint, and placed under a milk-vessel, was supposed to stop the contents from being spirited away. There were charms and rituals against almost every kind of ill a man, woman, child or beast could suffer, including aches, bruises and sprains, consumption and other diseases of the chest, toothache, warts, styes, herpes, whooping cough, hiccups, swollen glands and lumbago.

Stones had particular significance – bear stones and borestones; charm stones and healing stones; stones of destiny and stones of evil power. These were not just the huge objects, arranged in vast, mystic circles at which one can still gaze and wonder – such as the Ring of Brodgar and the Stenness Standing Stones in Orkney, Callanish in Lewis, the Clava Cairns by Inverness and, in the south, Torhouse Stone Circle by Wigtown. There are the medium-sized stones as well, of which the Stone of Destiny is the most notable example. By Strathpeffer, a village some five miles inland from the Cromarty Firth, is the Eagle Stone. It has been prophesied that ships will anchor to it when it has fallen three times. It has done so twice over the years, and its balance is now the object of continual surveillance.

Granny Kempock's Stone, on the cliff by Gourock, formed part of a ritual observed by fishermen to ensure fair weather. Betrothed couples also used to walk round it to obtain the spirit's blessing. In the Dee near Dinnet was once a stone with a hole in it, by squeezing through which a childless wife could become a joyful mother. One aristocratic lady tried, with no success. She had gone through the wrong way, against the stream. She tried again, in the correct direction, and achieved her aim. Some magic stones had life, as well as power and instinct. There was one in Birsay which, every Hogmanay night, when the clock struck twelve, marched to the nearby loch and stuck its head in the water. This was never actually proved, because anyone who tried to watch the stone's progress was found dead in the morning. Domestic stones were magic, too. The knocking-stone, roughly shaped into a bowl in which corn was bruised,

symbolised the luck of the home, as did the round stone on which bannocks were baked. These were always carried safely with the family when it moved house.

Then there were the little stones, which could fit comfortably into one's pocket, or be hung around one's neck. No one who has experienced the pleasure of holding a smooth pebble or piece of crystal in the palm of the hand can fail to understand how these, too, became endowed with magic power, to be passed from father to son, from mother to daughter, as charms against sickness, danger, misfortune, and the power of the evil eye. Such a family stone is the Lee Penny, a heart-shaped cornelian set in a silver coin. It was featured by Sir Walter Scott in his novel *The Talisman*, and was so famous for its healing properties that in the reign of Charles I it was hired by the city of Newcastle for £6000 during an epidemic of the plague.

Particular places have magical associations, too, like the Moot Hill at Scone, to which, at the crowning of a king of Scotland, every chief and noble brought a handful of earth to spread on the ground and stand on while he swore the oath of allegiance. Fairy hills abound – like Schiehallion in the Grampians and Tom-na-hurich in Inverness. Even Edinburgh's Calton Hill has fairy connections: in a mansion beneath its slopes, the elves were said to hold a dance every Thursday. And it was while he was taking his ease on the Eildon Hills that Thomas the Rhymer saw, and was enchanted and taken by, the Fairy Queen, who returned him to earth seven years later. The tradition and character of Thomas the Rhymer, poet and prophet, are probably based on a real person, Thomas of Erceldoune, who lived in the thirteenth century. There is absolutely no doubt, however, of the existence of Rev. Robert Kirk, author of *The Secret Commonwealth*, a serious and scholarly study of fairyland and its inhabitants. He studied at St Andrews and Edinburgh Universities, and was Minister of Balquhidder, and then Aberfoyle. He died, if he did die, in 1592, and his tomb was still to be seen in the churchyard in the time of Sir Walter Scott. But there was nothing in it. The tradition is that Kirk was 'removed' by the fairies because he knew too much. Fairy abductors seem to have worked overtime in Clackmannanshire. A miller in Menstrie lost his wife and for years just heard her voice in the house, singing a sad little verse:

O Alva hills is bonny
Tillicoultry hills is fair;
But to think on the braes o' Menstrie,
It makes my heart fu' sair.

One day, he was at the door of his mill when, instinctively or unwittingly, he adopted a magic posture. His wife promptly materialised in his arms. And the wife of a Tullibody blacksmith was actually taken up the chimney as he worked.

Scottish spirits and fairies come in all sorts of forms, shapes and sizes. Both mermen and mermaids are keen on obtaining human mates, and will use their power of enchantment to seduce away a member of the opposite sex.

Selkies, the seal-folk who inhabit the sea round Orkney and Shetland, are of a different kind. A selkie can put off his or her skin and appear on land in human form. Many are the stories of island men seeing beautiful girls disporting themselves naked on the shore, and creeping up to take and hide a skin. Until the skin was found, the seal-maiden had to be the man's wife or, in some versions, his mistress. Uricks are spirits of the forest, in a form which is half-man, half-goat. Brownies, who frequent the Lowlands, are helpful, domesticated creatures. Not so the kelpie, a malevolent water-spirit in the form of a horse, which can assume human shape at will. A typical kelpie ploy is to lure a tired traveller on to its back, and then plunge into a deep loch.

The distinction between the belief in supernatural rites for protection against misfortune and for the cure of ills, and their supposed use for evil purposes, is so fine that it is little surprise that a superstitious society often could not appreciate it. In 1563, the Scottish Parliament established witchcraft as a secular crime, opening the door to large-scale witch hunts. Though the last execution under the Act was in 1722, that did not prevent the belief in witchcraft lingering on – the last great auk recorded in Scotland was found on St Kilda in 1821, captured alive, tied up for three days, and then clubbed to death as a suspected witch!

The most extensive witch hunt of all took place in 1590, and involved the King, James VI, and the Earl of Bothwell, nephew and heir of the third husband of Mary, Queen of Scots. Over a hundred people were arrested. It all started with rumours that a servant girl called Gilly Duncan was claiming that she knew how to cure sicknesses. To her employer, and to others, that could only spell witchcraft. Her body was minutely examined, and a tiny birthmark found which was pronounced to be 'the devil's mark'. Under the most unimaginable torture, the girl confessed to witchcraft and named several others, including Agnes Sampson, known as the Wise Woman of Keith. James VI ordered Agnes to be brought to the Palace of Holyroodhouse and himself presided at her examination. After being kept without sleep and tortured, Agnes finally confessed that, on the preceding All Hallow's Eve, she and two hundred other witches and warlocks had set sail in a fleet of sieves, making merry and drinking wine (out of sieves), and had landed at North Berwick, where Gilly Duncan had led them dancing to the churchyard as she played a reel on a Jew's harp. James called for Gilly, who demonstrated her ability on that instrument. Almost all those implicated were burned alive, or strangled and then burned, even those who strenuously denied all charges. The Earl of Bothwell, who certainly was plotting to overthrow the King, escaped from prison in Edinburgh Castle and, after making a thorough nuisance of himself, finally got away to the Continent in 1595.

Where the Castle Esplanade turns into Castlehill, there is a bronze tablet and fountain marking the spot where, between 1479 and 1722, three hundred women were burned as witches. None of them was more unfortunate than Lady Glamis, widow of the sixth Lord, who was convicted of the improbable charge of the 'imagination of the slaughter and destruction ... by poison' of James V, and burned in 1537.

The death sentence on her son on the same charge was commuted to life imprisonment, but he was released on James's death five years later, thus enabling the line to continue.

Lady Glamis is said to haunt the clock tower of Glamis Castle, the seat of the Earls of Strathmore and Kinghorne. Sir Walter Scott visited the castle as a young man, and was struck by its strange atmosphere and by the revelation that there was a hidden room, the secret entrance to which was known only to the Earl and his heir. People have tried to find it ever since. From this tradition derives the rumour that the room contains the Monster of Glamis, or other ghostly occupants. The novelist Mrs Oliphant wrote a story about it, called *The Secret Chamber*, which was published in 1886.

Other Scottish ghosts, and there are many, tend to be more conventional. Bonnie Prince Charlie haunts Culloden House, and also a hotel in Dumfries. Mary, Queen of Scots, is supposed to have been seen in the Palace of Holyroodhouse, Craigmillar Castle, Hermitage Castle, and (dressed as a boy) Borthwick Castle, while one of her attendants is said to be the Green Lady of Stirling Castle. Perhaps not surprisingly, a tall, handsome, ghostly figure has been seen at Ardvreck Castle, where Montrose was betrayed. Edinburgh has many ghosts, the most notorious being Major Weir, a self-confessed warlock, who admitted also adultery, bestiality and incest, and was burned in 1670 at the age of seventy-one. He gallops up and down High Street on a headless black horse. Ann Street, in the New Town, boasts two ghosts of a gentler kind. The Grey Lady, in eighteenth-century dress, glides along the street, occasionally entering a house to stand silently by the bed of an occupant. Number 12 was once owned by the Swan family, whose son was sent away to sea and died of homesickness. He returned as a ghost, was exorcised, and disappeared. In 1936, when new owners moved in, he came back for three years, during which time he was referred to by the children as 'the little man in black, who comes to say good-night'.

Edinburgh's most famous supernatural being is the ghostly herald who appeared at the Mercat Cross the night before Flodden, and solemnly read out a list of those who were to die in the battle, beginning with the King. Some Scottish instances of second sight, or 'two sights' (which is the meaning of the Gaelic term), are too well authenticated for the phenomenon to be dismissed. Among the more extraordinary predictions are those of the Brahan Seer, believed by some to be an amalgam of unnamed prophets, and by others to have been Kenneth Mackenzie, better known as Coinneach Odhar, said to have been executed on the orders of the wife of his patron, the third Earl of Seaforth, to whom he had under protest suggested that her husband had left her for a French lady of fashion. As he died, Coinneach prophesied all sorts of disasters for the family, which duly descended on its members. Enough of the other prophecies attributed to the Brahan Seer have been fulfilled to suggest genuine second sight on the part of whoever made them. Among those which have not yet happened is the extermination of animal life in the Highlands by 'horrid black rain'. Could this be a reference to oil pollution?

Glasgow

Glasgow was founded in about A.D. 543 by St Mungo – he was also known as Kentigern, which means 'High Lord'. His parentage goes back to the time of the legendary King Arthur, if not also into Arthurian legend itself. His father was supposed to have been Owen, King of Strathclyde, nephew of Arthur, and his mother, Thaneu, daughter of one of Arthur's chiefs and sister of the traitor Modred. Thaneu's own people, suspecting, or seeing evidence of, her adultery, set her adrift in the Firth of Clyde in a coracle which, instead of sailing out to sea, floated upstream and landed her at Culross, where Mungo was born.

The boy trained as a priest in the Celtic Church under St Serf at the monastery at Culross. He appears to have been a precocious pupil, given to performing miracles, and was his teacher's pet. This made him unpopular, and he left. Finding himself one day at the home of Fergus, a holy man, he decided to pay him a visit. Now Fergus had been told in a dream that he would not die until he had set eyes on the man who would be the country's saviour. The moment Mungo came into the hut, Fergus knew him to be the one. He said a prayer, and then expired. The next morning, Mungo miraculously found two wild bulls grazing quietly outside. He yoked them to a cart, on which he placed the holy man's body, and let them trundle off with their strange load, resolving to follow them wherever they should go. They finally stopped thirty miles away, on the banks of the Molendinar Burn. Here, at a spot which Mungo called 'Glasgu' – dear green place –, he buried Fergus and established a church. The name was prophetic, for visitors to Glasgow today cannot fail to be impressed by the spirit of 'togetherness' which the inhabitants display (and which has motivated them for centuries), and the greenness of parks and avenues which belies the city's traditional image as a grimy centre of industry.

Mungo's church grew into an ecclesiastical complex with a school, monastery, library and visitors' accommodation, and became the religious centre of Strathclyde. In the succeeding Dark Ages, all these disappeared, until David, son of Malcolm III and Prince of Strathclyde, restored to the church in 1118 the lands it had originally held. When he became King, a new cathedral to the memory of St Mungo was consecrated in 1136, but it was destroyed by fire. A replacement, built by Bishop Jocelyn, was consecrated in 1197. At this time, Glasgow was a market town, which had grown up on either side of the series of streets which ran one after the other, as they still do, from the Cathedral to a bridge over the Clyde. Jocelyn received, from King William the Lion, royal assent to the holding every year of the Glasgow Fair, which is still celebrated as a holiday.

The present Cathedral largely dates from the great rebuilding done in the time of Bishop William de Bondington 1233-58, while the steeple dates from about 1420. There are two levels, and in the lower section is the tomb of St Mungo with, nearby, a carving on a stone of two oxen and a cart, and an inscription naming the aisle as that of Fergus. Robert Wishart (Bishop from 1271 to 1316) was one of those fighting clerics, supporting and often leading the cause of Robert the Bruce against Edward I. He was captured in 1306 and imprisoned. When he was released after the Battle of Bannockburn, he was blind. On his official seals, we find for the first time the four devices which appear on the armorial insignia of Glasgow – the bird, the upside-down salmon with a ring in its mouth, the tree and the bell. All are associated with St Mungo. The bird belonged to his teacher, St Serf, and was miraculously restored to life by Mungo after it had been killed by his fellow-pupils. The tree represents the hazel branch which burst conveniently into flames in his hands after the same pupils had hoped to embarrass him by dousing the holy fire in the refectory while he was in charge of it. The bell is that which the Pope gave him on a trip to Rome. The ring and the fish recall a faintly improper story. King Roderick of Strathclyde, suspecting his Queen, Languoreth, of having an affair with one of his knights, rifled the man's pockets while he slept off the effects of a hunting picnic Roderick had organised. Finding a ring which he himself had given to her, Roderick threw it into the Clyde. He then threatened Languoreth with death if she could not produce it. Her lover was no help, of course. In a right tizzy, she appealed to Mungo to do something. He calmed her down, and sent one of his monks to the river with a fishing line and orders to bring back the first fish he caught. Sure enough, in its mouth was the ring.

While Bishop Wishart was held in prison, the Bishop of Durham came with a thousand knights and occupied his residence, known as the Bishop's Castle. A furious William Wallace, who regarded himself as the saviour of Scotland, resolved to get it back. He rode through the night from Ayr to Glasgow with three hundred men, half of whom he sent round to the slope above the Castle. He then marched up the High Street towards the Castle at the head of the rest, making warlike noises. The English surged out in force, and met him at Bell o' the Brae, where George Street joins the High Street today. Wallace's men were creating dreadful carnage in the narrow street when, suddenly, their colleagues came charging down the hill, took the unsuspecting English in the rear, and completed a famous victory.

Glasgow University was the second of the four ancient Scottish seats of learning to be founded. The first was St Andrews, established by Bishop Wardlaw in 1411 in his own cathedral city, an act of considerable ecclesiastical one-upmanship. James II, anxious to secure the support of William Turnbull, Bishop of Glasgow, in his continual struggle with his nobles, made Glasgow a royal Burgh and in 1451 got the Pope's permission for the foundation in Glasgow of another university, on the model of the University of Bologna, where the Pope himself had studied. The rivalry between the sees of St Andrews and Glasgow continued unabated. In the 1530s, Cardinal Beaton twice provoked Archbishop Dunbar of Glasgow by raising his cross to bless the people on Glasgow's territory. The row peaked in 1543 with a riot between the two clerics and their cross-bearers in Glasgow Cathedral itself, during which both crosses and a number of heads were broken.

The statue of John Knox, dominating the surroundings from the highest point of the Necropolis overlooking the Cathedral, symbolises the religious differences which are such a part of the history of Glasgow, as of Scotland itself. In 1538, John Kennedy and Jerome Russell were burned at the stake outside the Cathedral for questioning Catholic doctrine. After the Reformation, it was the Catholics' turn to suffer. A priest called John Ogilvie was arrested on suspicion of plotting a revolution. He was tortured, but confessed nothing. He was taken from the Tolbooth in 1615 and hanged in the street outside for claiming that the Pope s authority transcended that of the King. After the defeat of Montrose at Philiphaugh in 1645, three of his particular friends were beheaded by the Covenanters in Glasgow, after surrendering under promise of mercy. And in 1684, five Covenanters, citizens of Glasgow, were hanged at the Mercat Cross. There is a memorial to them, and to four others executed for the same cause, on the outside wall of the Cathedral sacristy.

Of all the places in Scotland which had grim associations for Mary, Queen of Scots, Glasgow probably headed the list. In 1544, when she was just a baby, it was the scene of the Battle of the Butts, fought to the last between the forces of the earls of Arran and Lennox, each of whom claimed the right to rule on her behalf. Arran prevailed on that occasion, but his men then went on the rampage through the city, burning and killing. In 1566, she stayed at Provand's Lordship, the house that still stands near the Cathedral, while her husband Darnley was recovering from smallpox at his father's house in the city. There she probably wrote to Bothwell some of the notorious 'casket letters' that contributed to her ultimate execution; and from there she persuaded Darnley to return with her to Edinburgh, and to his death. And in 1568, from a spot on a hill by Cathcart Castle which is now marked by a carved stone, she watched the pike-ranks of the Earl of Moray, her own half-brother and Regent of Scotland, stand firm against everything her own forces could throw at them, and then move aside to let the Highlanders behind them charge through to utter victory. The rout that is known as the Battle of Langside took just forty-five minutes. Then Mary got on her horse and rode to England to throw herself on the mercy of her cousin Elizabeth. She never saw Scotland again.

In 1650, Cromwell defeated the Scottish Presbyterian army under General Leslie, the very man who had triumphed at Philiphaugh. When Cromwell entered Glasgow at the head of his troops, there was no one to greet him. All the magistrates and chief citizens had taken refuge in a castle nearby. He duly routed them out, and treated them with unexpected respect. One of the few who had stayed at their posts was Zachary Boyd, minister of the Barony Church, to which Cromwell went for service. Boyd treated him to a vitriolic sermon, which so incensed one of Cromwell's aides that he would have shot the preacher on the spot but for Cromwell's intervention. Instead, Boyd was invited to dinner, after which Cromwell led the company in prayers for three hours, while Boyd knelt on the stone floor. On

hearing, at the University, that Charles I had promised £200 to the library, but never paid it, Cromwell not only handed over that sum, but added a further £500.

One of Cromwell's camp followers wrote: 'The town of Glasgow, though not so big or so rich, yet to all seems a much sweeter and more delightful place than Edinburgh.' And Daniel Defoe, who visited the city in about 1720, recorded: 'It is one of the cleanliest, most beautiful, and best built cities in Great Britain.' It had not always been so. In 1589, the magistrates ordered that no 'midding' (refuse) should be thrown into the High Street. No one took much notice, as the practice continued at least for another hundred years. Things were little better indoors. According to Sir William Brereton in 1634: 'I could never pass through [a] hall but I was customed to hold my nose – their chambers, vessels, linen and meat very slovenly.' In 1655, those living on the north side of the Trongate had to import stepping-stones in order to cross the sewage which flowed between the street and their houses. Even as late as 1795 a petition was presented to the magistrates praying (unsuccessfully) that all haystacks in the Trongate should be removed.

Bonnie Prince Charlie's visit over the New Year 1746, on his retreat from Derby, was a spectacular affair. The city, having raised two battalions of volunteers to oppose him, had reason to be apprehensive. However, he merely fined the city £10,000, and demanded 12,000 shirts, and 6,000 coats, waistcoats, bonnets, and pairs of stockings and shoes, with which he re-equipped his Highlanders who, after five months on the march, were looking somewhat scruffy. Then, after ten days of moderate merriment – he dined twice a day in public, wearing a tartan silk jacket and crimson velvet breeches – and making the acquaintance of Clementina Walkinshaw, he organised a grand parade of his army and led them away to victory at Falkirk, but defeat at Culloden.

Glasgow was now a prosperous city of twenty thousand inhabitants, most of whom were crammed into the ten streets and seventeen wynds (alleys) which comprised the whole town. The Act of Union of 1707 had been bad for Scottish politics, but good for Glasgow business. Scots could now trade where English merchants had previously had a monopoly, and the Clyde was the most convenient point in Britain from which to sail to the new colonies in America and the West Indies. By the 1770s, the population had doubled, and a new class of plutocrats had surfaced, the Tobacco Lords, who made their wealth by importing sugar, rum and tobacco, and exporting on the return run goods for sale to those who ran the plantations. They wore distinctive dress, and appropriated for themselves the only pavement in the city, a stretch in front of the Tolbooth known as the Plainstanes. When the American War of Independence blew up in 1775, however, the Tobacco Lords were ruined, and vanished as quickly as they had come.

Lost fortunes were temporarily retrieved in the cotton factories (most of those in Scotland were in or around Glasgow), only to disappear again when America, the main source of the raw cotton, was plunged into the Civil War of the 1860s. Glasgow's greatness was revived by the deposits in the surrounding countryside of coal and iron ore, and by the inventiveness and skill of its engineers. A vast industry developed, building not only ships, but also railway engines, which were said to run on every railway line in the world, including those of India and China. Glasgow was truly the 'Second City of the Empire', and the sixth in Europe. By 1880, the population numbered over five hundred thousand, and the city was the progenitor of an incomparable Victorian architecture, as well as having one of the most notorious slums in Europe, the Gorbals. The industry collapsed when the coal and iron ore began to run out. It was no longer cheaper to build in Glasgow, and when ships and locomotives were required that ran on diesel oil, too few Glasgow yards had adapted to the change.

Traditional Glasgow entertainments survived for a bit longer, however. The first theatre in the city, a wooden structure, was built against the old castle wall in 1752, but was burned down the following year by a mob incited by a ranting preacher. Indeed, at one time or another, almost every Glasgow theatre has been burned down, some several times, by accident or by fanatics who regarded theatres as homes of the Devil. The hey-day of the music hall, a particularly Glaswegian institution, began in the latter half of the nineteenth century, and was triumphantly carried on by such giants of the boards as Sir Harry Lauder, Will Fyffe, Tommy Lorne, Harry Gordon and the like, who made the Christmas pantomime an annual pilgrimage for Glaswegians and visitors from all over Scotland.

Today, there is a new sense of purpose about this most cosmopolitan of Scottish cities. Much (much too much, according to the conservationists) of the Victorian architecture has been swept away in the interests of development and progress – only the sad modern tower-blocks really offend the eye, standing as monuments to misplaced, and misinformed, bureaucracy. Though the tramcars, which, soon after the change in 1902 from being horse-drawn to electrically-operated, carried over two hundred million passengers a year, are long gone, and the famous Glasgow Underground, opened in 1886, was replaced in 1979 by the Subway, the motorways which score their way across and around the city make car travel a genuine option. And families, who were once being persuaded to leave the city to settle in the new towns outside, are now being encouraged to return, to good living conditions and surroundings, and to jobs in the newer, smaller industries. Glasgow is also now a centre of finance, and the headquarters of several British national organisations.

Tourism has become a viable proposition. Glasgow has been the home of Scottish Opera since 1975, holds an annual international festival of arts (Mayfest), hosted the National Garden Festival in 1988, and has been designated European City of Culture for 1990. Those who so recently were hailed as philistines have justifiable cause for jubilation and pride. And of all that Glasgow has to offer the visitor, two things must not be missed. An annex to the Hunterian Art Gallery on Hillhead Street contains, on three floors, a reconstruction of the cool, spare interior of the house of Charles Rennie Mackintosh, that genius of design and architecture whose work is more appreciated now than ever before. Pollok Park is host to the Burrell Collection, a purpose-built, compact musem housing the fruits of a lifetime's selective collecting, and often bargaining, by Sir William Burrell, who retired from the family shipping business during the First World War, and spent the rest of his life (he died in 1958 at the age of ninety-six), and most of his fortune, on his hobby and consuming interest. The range is wide, and the exhibits are frequently changed. Every section contains at least one surprise, even for the regular visitor, and at least one utterly exquisite item.

Edinburgh

Din Eidyn means 'fortress of the hill-slopes' – *din* or *dun* was the equivalent of the Old English *burh*, meaning 'town'. The Castle rock itself is part of the core of one of the five extinct volcanoes in the area, and with three of its sides shorn almost sheer by the depredations of the Ice Age, and the fourth easily defensible, it made an ideal site for a fortress. Malcolm III's Queen Margaret, with her English ideas of civilised living, made the place into a residence as well, and it was here that they brought to her, in 1093, the news of the violent deaths of both her husband and her eldest son, who had been with him. The shock was too much, and she died three days later attended by her three other sons, who were all in their teens. Malcolm's brother Donald, claiming the Crown under Scottish law, immediately laid siege to the Castle. Duncan, Malcolm's son by his first marriage, and the rightful heir, was only slightly slower into the field. At a time when there were only two reliable ways of ensuring succession, by killing off your rivals or by blinding them (as subsequently happened to Duncan himself), the boys opted for retreat. Under cover of a convenient fog, they spirited themselves and their mother's body out through a secret postern in the western wall, and from there to Dunfermline, where she was buried.

Since then, the Castle has on several occasions changed hands as the result of siege. It has never, however, been entered by force, though twice it was won back from the English by stealth or subterfuge. In 1313, a Frenchman called William informed Thomas Randolph, nephew of Robert I, that when stationed in the Castle as a young man, he had been in the habit of climbing down the rock face after lights out to visit a girl friend in the town. He duly led Randolph's party up the rock, and they scaled the Castle wall with a rope-ladder and expelled the invaders. The English returned in due course, but were removed again in 1341 by William of Douglas, who disguised himself and his companions as merchants bringing provisions. As their cart entered the gate, they shoved their load on to the ground, jamming it open. Whereupon a band of armed men, hidden in the approaches, dashed through. The whole garrison, forty-nine men-at-arms, six watchmen and sixty mounted archers, surrendered.

Escaping from the Castle was equally difficult. The Duke of Albany succeeded in 1479 by getting his guards drunk, throwing them on the fire, and then abseiling down the rock on twisted sheets. In 1681, the Earl of Argyll, under sentence of death, managed to walk out disguised as his daughter-in-law's footman. The infant James II, locked up in the Castle by William Crichton, was abducted in a box with air holes. His mother had announced she was going on a pilgrimage. The box was carried out as part of her luggage. In 1440, when he was ten, James was an innocent and tearful spectator of the most infamous deed perpetrated within the Castle precincts, known as the Black Dinner. Crichton and his crony, Alexander Livingstone, the joint Regents, invited the young Earl of Douglas, whose power they feared, to dine with them and the King. During the meal, Douglas and his brother were seized, taken out into the courtyard, and beheaded.

It was in the Castle, whose Great Hall he built, that James IV had his master-gunner build the seventeen huge cannon which were laboriously dragged to Flodden – the journey of forty-eight miles took a fortnight. After the defeat, the Town Council, fearing an English attack, ordered a defensive wall to be built immediately, right round the city. It was finished forty-seven years later! Mons Meg, the even vaster cannon which still adorns the Castle, was fired from the walls to celebrate the marriage of Mary, Queen of Scots, to the Dauphin – the ball was found two miles away and brought back for re-use. And in the tiny, odd-shaped, oak-panelled chamber off Queen Mary's Room, she gave birth to James VI in 1566. In 1573, the Castle was held in Mary's name by its Governor, Sir William Kirkcaldy, against the supporters of the cause of James for King, who were bolstered by fifteen hundred men and thirty siege guns sent by Queen Elizabeth. Only lack of food, water and ammunition, and threats by some of his less-determined men, persuaded Kirkcaldy finally to surrender. By contrast, the last defence of the Castle, in 1745, was entirely successful. Bonnie Prince Charlie blockaded its exit, but thought better of his action and withdrew the guard when the commander of the Castle opened fire with cannon-shot, killing four people in the town.

Today, just as then, there is only one way out of the Castle. This leads into the Royal Mile, that single road made up of four streets, one after the other, which culminates in the Abbey Strand and the gates of Holyroodhouse. Castlehill, the scene of the witch-burnings, gives way to Lawnmarket, and, where Lawnmarket joins High Street, three brass strips in the road mark the spot where the last public hanging took place in 1864. Set back from the road is Parliament House, where the Scottish Parliament sat from 1640 to its demise in 1707. The crown of St Giles' Cathedral is some five hundred years old, though some parts of the building are much older. It once housed four separate churches, each one offering a different form of service, and from the pulpit of one of these John Knox thundered out his tirades against Catholicism in general and Mary, Queen of Scots, in particular. The Cathedral was the scene, too, in 1637, of the riot against Charles I's order of service, begun when Jenny Geddes threw her stool at the Dean. St Giles' did not always dominate the street as it does today. Until 1817, a range of buildings completely obscured its north front and reduced the width of the street to a few yards. At the west end of the range was

the Tolbooth, with spikes set into its roof for the heads of executed prisoners. The other buildings were known as the Luckenbooths, and comprised a row of shops with tenements above. In the reminiscences of Henry Mackenzie (1745-1831) is the account of the crack golfer who wagered that from one of the windows at the east end of the Luckenbooths he could reach the top of Arthur's Seat (a distance of about a mile and a half, if played as a dog-leg, to a point 823 feet high) in six strokes, playing his first out of a stone basin. He won his bet!

At the bottom of High Street, brass studs in the road mark the site of the Netherbow Port (Gate), set in the Flodden Wall. Through this gate, from Parliament House, whatever Sir Walter Scott's poem about him suggests to the contrary, rode Graham of Claverhouse ('Bonny Dundee') to raise the Highlands for James VII. And through it, from the opposite direction, burst Bonnie Prince Charlie's Highlanders to win the city without violence. They cunningly chose the moment when the portcullis was raised to let the driver of the coach, which had just taken back to the city the Town Council's envoys, return to his stables in Canongate.

Canongate itself is so called because it was the gait (way) the canons of the Abbey of Holyroodhouse took on their way to and from the old St Mary's Church in Edinburgh Castle. The Abbey was founded in 1128 by David I, youngest son of Malcolm III and Margaret. The story goes that he was hunting on the lower slopes of Arthur's Seat, which was then covered in forest, when a stag charged, unseating him and wounding him in the thigh. As he fell, David grabbed at the stag's horns, and found he was holding a crucifix, which remained in his hands as the stag made off. That night, in a dream, he was instructed to build an abbey and monastery near the site of his accident. Holyroodhouse means 'house of the holy cross'. While the Abbey was being built, a stone-carver fell from the roof and was killed outright. The body was wrapped in a winding sheet and left in front of the altar, where David found it. He knelt and prayed, and then ordered a mass to be said. When the cloth was drawn back from the corpse's face, the man was found to be alive again. In this Abbey, in 1503, James IV married the twelve-year-old Magaret Tudor, bringing together the royal houses of Scotland and England. Less happily, it was the scene, too, of the weddings of Mary, Queen of Scots, first to Lord Darnley, and then to the Earl of Bothwell. The Abbey was used as a parish church until James VII insisted on refurbishing it for Catholic worship. After he had fled to France, an angry mob broke in and wrecked the place, even desecrating the royal burial vault. It has not been used for worship since. The roof collapsed in 1788, but the vault was restored on the command of Queen Victoria, and in it lie the bones of David II; James II and his Queen, Mary of Gueldres; James V and first wife, Magdalene of France; and Lord Darnley.

The Palace was originally the Abbey guest house, enlarged by James IV, who built the great northwest tower, which still stands today, and in which Mary, Queen of Scots, had her apartments. She arrived, ominously, in thick fog, in August 1561, and only when it cleared could she see the size of her palace, which was even more extensive than it is today. She married Darnley in 1565. His violent and jealous nature boiled over the following year, as Mary sat at dinner one night in her apartments with her Italian secretary, and favourite, David Rizzio, and other members of her household. Darnley and several other armed men crept up the secret staircase to the room, dragged Rizzio, screaming, from his seat and stabbed him violently and repeatedly – it is said, fifty-six times. It is significant that when Mary persuaded Darnley to return with her from Glasgow after his bout of smallpox, he was not lodged in the Palace, but in a house at Kirk-o'-Field some distance away, where she had had a bedroom furnished for him on the first floor. Some nights, she slept in the room immediately below his, but not on 9 February 1567. At two o'clock in the morning, an explosion blew the house apart. The bodies of Darnley and his page were later discovered in the garden. Both had been strangled!

On 26 March 1603, James VI went early to bed in the Palace, tired of waiting for news that never came. Then a horseman, covered with mud, and bruised by a heavy fall, clattered into the courtyard. Reeling with fatigue, he was ushered into the royal bedroom. Sir Robert Carey had ridden the 397 miles from Richmond in sixty hours with the news that Elizabeth was dead, and he showed one of her rings to prove it. With James's departure for London, there was a lapse in glittering occasions, but in 1661, after the Restoration, a joyful Scottish Parliament collected, from the various towns that had them, all the bits of the body of Montrose that could be found eleven years after his execution, put them in a coffin, and gave him a splendid Abbey funeral. Royalty, of a kind, was in residence in 1745 in the form of Bonnie Prince Charlie, who for seven weeks made spectacular celebration, with banquets, soirées, receptions and balls. Since 1850, the Palace has seen regular state visits by the royal family, and these have now become annual occasions.

The Old Town of Edinburgh, enclosed by the Flodden wall on three sides and on the fourth by the Nor' Loch (an even earlier defensive measure), and surrounded by marshy ground too treacherous for building on, was one of the most crowded and insanitary places in Europe. A maze of narrow alleys (closes, wynds, or vennels) spread out like veins or tentacles down the sides of the rocky spine which carried the main street from the Castle to the Netherbow Port. Slim, rickety tenement blocks, some of them fifteen storeys high, were crammed together, their tops leaning over so far that one could shake hands with the person living opposite. These blocks were known as 'lands', and often housed, on separate floors, noblemen, tradesmen, professional people, and beggars, the upper and bottom floors being regarded as the less desirable. Until 1681, when water started to be piped to Edinburgh, it had to be carried upstairs in heavy casks from one of the wells around the city. It was the standard practice simply to hurl refuse and the contents of one's chamber pots out of the window into the street, with just a cry of 'Gardy-Loo' (garde-l'eau) to warn passers-by what was afoot. As an unnamed baronet, a politician of some distinction, observed to James Boswell in about 1770, with a modicum of understatement, 'Walking in Edinburgh at night is pretty perilous, and a good deal oderiferous'. By about that time, however, work had already begun on a grandiose scheme which was to change the face of Edinburgh and make the city an architectural show-place.

The motivation came from George Drummond, first elected Lord Provost of Edinburgh in 1725. He had seen that if the Nor' Loch was drained, and a bridge constructed, there would be ready access to fields on the other side that were crying out to be built upon. In 1759, the loch was duly drained, leaving a dry valley covering an area from a point between the present North and Waverley Bridges to the far end of Princes Street Gardens. The foundation stone of the original North Bridge was laid in 1763 by Drummond himself, though there was as yet no detailed architect's plan for it. A bridge of sorts was opened to pedestrians in 1769, but it collapsed the same year, burying five people and cutting off the first public building to be erected on the opposite side, the Theatre Royal. The bridge was finally completed in 1772 (it was rebuilt 1896-97). With speculators (many of them city officials) buying up tracts of land, a competition was announced in 1766 for a design of the New Town. It was won by an unknown, twenty-three year-old architect, James Craig, nephew of the poet James Thomson. His prize was a gold medal and a silver box containing the freedom of the city.

Craig's plan was brilliant in its mathematical simplicity – two vast squares were linked by three main streets, with lesser streets joining them at right angles. The squares were to be named St Andrew's and St George's, after the patron saints of Scotland and England, but George III's Queen Charlotte is said to have proposed her name in place of that of St George. The royal couple were already enshrined in the names of George Street and Queen Street: the other main street was to be called St Giles'. The King, however, had apparently never heard of Edinburgh's patron saint, so it was renamed Princes Street after a pair of royal sinners, the future George IV and his brother, the Duke of York. Houses were to be built on the north side of Princes Street only, so that there would be an unrestricted view of the gardens and the Castle. This intention was re-affirmed by a judgment in the House of Lords against the Town Council for attempting to do otherwise, and confirmed by Act of Parliament in 1814.

Even though the brothers Robert and James Adam had been commissioned to design Register House and a complete frontage for Charlotte Square, people were slow to take advantage of the new possibilities. Indeed, the Town Council had to offer a prize of £20 to the first individual to start to build there. It was won by John Young, who got James Craig himself to lay the foundation stone of his house off George Street. There were rules for the design of all buildings. No house on a main street could be higher than three storeys, and the front of each should be level with that next to it – regulations today ensure that when houses and blocks of flats in the New Town are repaired or renovated, they retain their original aspect. By the end of the eighteenth century, the New Town had become a fashionable place in which to live, but not necessarily to work – when William Blackwood moved his publishing business from the Old Town to Princes Street in 1816, even his competitors doubted his sanity. Soon, however, the New Town was being extended to the north, to the east, where it took in Calton Hill, the third of the seven hills of Edinburgh to be incorporated in the city, and to the west, where Thomas Telford built the sensational bridge across the Water of Leith.

Edinburgh, with the Castle, Palace, remnants and basic structures of parts of the Old Town, and the splendid, Georgian dignity of the New Town, is a city of living history. It has been lucky, too, in the writers who have chronicled its progress, personalities and appearance through the ages. It is still the capital of Scotland and the centre of the government and law. Its two universities are at the forefront of research in medicine and science, and it is the home of the National Library of Scotland (one of the six copyright libraries in the United Kingdom), national galleries and museums, and a zoo which has deservedly won international fame. The annual Edinburgh Festival, founded in 1947 at the height of Britain's period of austerity, is still, despite frequent wrangles and financial crises, one of the key events in the international cultural circuit, and through its 'Fringe' entertainments has been a stage for hosts of hitherto unknown actors, writers and performers.

Palaces and Castles

The oldest Scottish royal palace of which any part still exists was originally the guest-house of Dunfermline Abbey, established by Malcolm's Queen Margaret with the standard number, at that time, of thirteen monks. Thus, it is perfectly understandable that in the opening line of the famous ballad of *Sir Patrick Spens*, 'The King sits in Dunfermline toun ...'. The Stewarts enlarged the building considerably, and it was regularly used as a royal residence right up to the time of James VI. Indeed, both Charles I and his sister Elizabeth, from whom the present royal family is descended, were born there.

In medieval times, royal households were continually on the move. They went round to supervise the running of the royal estates, to consume the rents that were paid in kind, and to enable the last port of call to be cleaned up. The presence of a large party in one place for any length of time put a strain on the primitive sanitary arrangements. Linlithgow had been the site of a royal manor house since the time of David I. It was burned down in 1424, whereupon James I embarked upon the building of a splendid replacement, which became an occasional, and welcome, home for several of his successors. James IV settled on his English bride the lordship of Linlithgow – palace, town, and all – and it was in the Palace that he is believed to have said goodbye to her and their baby son before Flodden. James V's Queen, Mary of Guise, who knew many of the great houses of France, said that she had never seen a more princely palace than Linlithgow. Their daughter Mary, Queen of Scots, was born there, and lived in the Palace with her widowed mother for the first seven months of her life.

James VI even held a Parliament in the Palace in 1585 – a throwback to the ancient tradition that it sat where the King should happen to be. The last monarch to sleep in the Palace was Charles I, in 1633, but Cromwell lived there for part of the winter of 1650-51, spending much of the time having fortifications built. On 31 January 1746, some of Cumberland's troops were billeted in the Palace on their way from Edinburgh to fight Bonnie Prince Charlie. The housekeeper complained to their commander, General Hawley, that the huge fires they had lit around the place were dangerous, and when she got no satisfaction, remarked: 'Aweel, aweel, I can rin frae fire as fast as ony general.' Her concern was justified. The fires were left burning when the soldiers departed in the morning, and ignited the straw on which they had slept. The present building is all that remained from the conflagration.

The Palace of Falkland on the other side of the Forth was the favourite house of the unhappy Stewart monarchs, and still belongs to the Crown. The Stewarts came to relax, to hunt the stags and wild boar in the surrounding forests, to hawk with falcons on the hills, to practise archery and play tennis – the present court was built by James V. James II transformed the old castle and built the North Range, and after his accidental death in a cannon explosion, his wife, to whom he had given the burgh of Falkland on their marriage, and who was Regent for their son, lived there and built a room for herself leading on to a private garden. James III, when he grew up, probably built the Great Hall, in which he invited leading musicians of the day to play. James IV inherited his father's interest in architecture and the arts, and built the South and the East ranges, in which were the royal apartments. James V improved the South Range, which houses the Chapel Royal, employing French master masons to carve the local stone of the façade into one of the most exquisite examples of Renaissance architecture in Britain. His widow, Mary of Lorraine, lived on there, and their daughter Mary, Queen of Scots, used to come with her husband regularly from 1561 to 1565, to get away from affairs of state. It may even be her hand which carved the name MARIE STUART in a window recess in the Chapel, uncovered in the nineteenth century. Her son, James VI, lived somewhat hazardously at Falkland. In 1582, when fifteen, he was kidnapped by the first Earl of Gowrie, who ruled in his name with two other earls who were in the plot. Restored to Falkland a year later, but still under unwelcome surveillance, James escaped to friends in St Andrews. In 1592, the Earl of Bothwell (the 'witch hunt' one, not the beau of Mary, Queen of Scots) arrived in Falkland with three hundred horsemen in an attempt to capture the King by forcing a tiny gate in the East Range. The results of his diversionary tactic of raking the main gate with heavy musket-fire can still be seen in the form of bullet holes. And in 1600, there was another attempt to kidnap James, by the grandson of the first Earl of Gowrie, who lured him from Falkland to Huntingtower Castle with a trumped-up story.

It is with the death of James V at Falkland, however, and his prophecy about the Stewart line, that the Palace is most indelibly associated. It was also the scene, in 1528, of his daring escape from the attentions of the troublesome Douglases, who were keeping the sixteen-year-old King under close guard while they exercised power in the land. The place was so heavily guarded that two attempts to rescue him by force had failed. One evening, James announced that he would go hunting the next day, and retired early to bed. As the lights were being doused through the Palace, two grooms were seen making their way to the stables. No one thought anything of it, as the horses' tackle would need to be got ready for the morning. One of the grooms, however, was the King, and there was a servant with fast horses waiting behind the stables. Early next morning, the sheriff of nearby Abernethy appeared at the palace gates, asking to see the King. The Douglas in charge of the household explained that he was still in his room. 'Not so,' replied the sheriff. 'He crossed Stirling Bridge at daybreak!' The royal guard sprang to their horses and gave pursuit. It was too late. James was among his supporters in Stirling Castle; the gates were closed and the drawbridge raised. And a royal edict had been pronounced, banning any Douglas from coming within six miles of the King's presence.

Stirling Castle was a 'safe house' by any standards, akin to Edinburgh Castle in the rugged eminence of its position over the town, as well as its historical and royal associations. No traces remain of the original castle, but Alexander I and William I died there, as did David, second son of Alexander III, whose death at the age of eight in 1291 and that of his elder brother four years later precipitated the War of Independence. When Edward I of England came in 1304 with his stone-throwing artillery, the Castle proved such a tough nut to crack (though it was probably constructed mainly of wood), that he had to order lead to be stripped from the roofs of the Cathedrals of Dunblane and St Andrews, and from Dunfermline Abbey, to use as heavy ammunition, before he could batter it into surrender. The Castle guarded the main route between the north and south. It was still in English hands in 1313, but its governor agreed to surrender it to Edward Bruce, brother of Robert I, if it was not relieved by the English before mid-summer's day of the following year. Robert was not yet ready for a full-scale engagement, but he had to have Stirling Castle. On 24 June 1314, he completed, on the field of Bannockburn below the castle walls, a brilliant tactical victory over a much better-equipped and trained army more than twice the size of his.

The present castle dates from the second half of the fifteenth century. James IV was staying there in 1488, when the faction that was rebelling against his father took him out to be their figure-head at the Battle of Sauchieburn, after which James III was murdered. Remorse caused James IV to return frequently to pray in the Royal Chapel – he also wore a penitential iron belt for the rest of his life. He made merry as well, with elaborate hunting expeditions, tournaments, and exotic banquets, and entertained state and personal guests: among them Perkin Warbeck, pretender to the English throne, and Margaret Drummond, James's mistress and fiancée, and the mother of his child, born in 1497. Margaret and her two sisters died mysteriously of poisoning

in 1501. The next year, James signed the marriage contract binding him to his English princess. A more unusual guest was an alchemist called John Damian, who wormed his way into the King's confidence, but chanced his luck once too often when he announced he would fly from the battlements on wings of his own construction. He survived, complaining afterwards that he had unwittingly used feathers 'from barnyard and dunghill fowls', whose bent was naturally to the ground.

James V spent much of his childhood at Stirling, and later improved the defences and completed the palace quarters. His two sons died there in infancy, leaving his daughter Mary, Queen of Scots, as his sole heir. When she was just ten months old she was crowned in the Chapel, where twenty-four years later her son James was baptised. The following year he was crowned in the Parish Kirk of Stirling, and borne to the Castle in the arms of the Earl of Mar, its Governor. James VI's eldest son, Henry, was born and baptised in Stirling Castle, and spent nine years there being tutored. His death in 1612 at the age of nineteen left his younger brother, Charles, heir to the thrones of both Scotland and England.

The splendid ruins of Bothwell Castle mark one of the oldest surviving fortifications in Scotland, originally built in the thirteenth century, when Alexander's firm and enlightened government gave time and opportunity for construction programmes. In 1381, it came to the Douglas family by the marriage of its heiress to Archibald the Grim. His descendant, the sixth Earl of Douglas, succeeded to the title, and the Castle, when he was fourteen, and it was he and his brother who were murdered at Edinburgh Castle in the presence of James II. The eighth Earl actually met his death at the hands of James II, who stabbed him at Stirling Castle in 1452. Threave Castle is also associated with this branch of the family – known as the Black Douglases. It was built by Archibald the Grim, and at the time of the ninth Earl it was the last Douglas stronghold left, until James II razed it with a huge cannon. The Earl took refuge in England. When Threave was finally forfeited, it passed into the family of the Earls of Nithsdale, the fifth of whom was sentenced to death for his part in the 1715 Jacobite rebellion. The day before the execution, Lady Nithsdale visited him several times in the Tower of London, with one or more female companions. The guards, totally confused by all this coming and going, failed to notice that the woman who left with Lady Nithsdale towards dusk was not female, but his Lordship in drag.

Kildrummy Castle, east of Aberdeen, and Roxburghe Castle, in the Borders, share a grim part in the events following the accession of Robert I. The King had only a handful of supporters at this time, and the English were after him. He despatched the Queen and her ladies, and his sister Mary Bruce, to the mighty castle of Kildrummy, which was held by his brother Nigel, and himself took refuge in Rathlin, off the north coast of Ireland. On his return, there was news of the worst kind. Kildrummy had fallen and Nigel had been hanged. Though the Queen and some of her entourage had been taken to England as hostages,

Mary Bruce was now shut up in a cage in Roxburghe Castle. The Countess of Buchan, who had placed the crown on Robert's head at his coronation, fared even worse. The cage in which she was confined was, according to a contemporary chronicler, hung out in the open from one of the towers of Berwick Castle, and there she remained for four years until Edward II transferred her to a local nunnery.

Even earlier than Bothwell is the core of Rothesay Castle, in the island of Bute, built at the beginning of the thirteenth century by Walter the Steward, ancestor of Robert II. It was attacked and entered in 1230 by Norsemen, who hacked through the stone wall with axes, and caused much bloodshed within. The Castle did not finally return to Scottish hands until after the Battle of Largs, but it was later ceded to the English by the craven John Balliol. It was taken back again, and later chosen by Robert II as one of his residences. Robert III conferred the title of Duke of Rothesay on his eldest son, David, who fell into the hands of the Duke of Albany, the King's brother, and was starved to death at the castle at Falkland. David's younger brother became James I.

The horrible Duke of Albany also built Doune Castle, now one of the most complete remains of a medieval stronghold and home of the nobility. After he and his immediate male relatives were beheaded at Stirling Castle on the orders of James I, Doune was annexed to the Crown, but eventually passed into the hands of the Earls of Moray, to whom it still belongs. It is one of several castles associated with Mary, Queen of Scots, who visited it occasionally and gave her name to Queen Mary's Apartments, over the castle kitchens.

Dumbarton Castle recalls both the beginning and the end of Mary's personal links with Scotland. From here, she left for France in 1548, at the age of five, accompanied on the ship by her child companions, the four Maries, each from one of the country's leading families and born at the same time as herself. And it was to the safety of Dumbarton that she was aiming in 1568, when the Earl of Moray planted his troops in front of hers at Langside. Crookston Castle was where she and Darnley honeymooned in 1563. In 1566, she rode from Jedburgh to Hermitage Castle, the home of the Earl of Bothwell, and back the same day (a total distance of eighty miles), to visit Bothwell, who had been wounded in a fight with a brigand. The exertion (or the excitement of seeing him) brought on a severe attack of fever. In the same year, there was held at Craigmillar Castle the famous conference at which Mary's chief lords and advisers bargained with her for a solution to the problem of what to do about Darnley. Dunbar Castle is perhaps best known for the splendidly insouciant way in which 'Black Agnes', Countess of Dunbar, held it against the English in 1338, in the absence of her husband. It was also where Mary and Darnley retreated to let things die down after the murder of Rizzio. After Darnley's death, and Bothwell's acquittal of complicity in it, Bothwell asked for, and got, the gift of Dunbar Castle, and here he brought the (probably compliant) Queen in 1567, having abducted her on the road from Linlithgow to Holyrood. Later that year, she was imprisoned at Lochleven Castle (once used as a palace by Robert III), from which eleven months later she achieved her dramatic, romantic, but ultimately fruitless escape.

St Andrews Castle, built in about 1200, was also the Archbishop's Palace from 1472 to 1559. It was the site of a weird ecclesiastical contest in 1514, when three dignitaries each claimed the position of primate – Gavin Douglas, the poet, nominated by the Queen Mother, Margaret Tudor, now married to the Earl of Angus; John Hepburn, elected by the Chapter of St Andrews; and Andrew Foreman, recommended by the Pope. Douglas was first in possession of the Castle, but was ejected by the forces of Hepburn, who had to give way finally to Foreman, an expert in the art of the peaceful pursuit of ambition by means of bribery. A later archbishop was Cardinal Beaton, whose brutal assassination in the Castle in 1546 and the subsequent siege of the murderers were the opening shots in the struggle of the Reformation.

Farther up the east coast, and standing stark off the shore below Stonehaven, are the magnificent, and considerable, remains of Dunnottar Castle, once the property of the Earls Marischal of Scotland, and the scene of one of the nation's most daring defences and baffling enigmas. When Charles II was crowned King in Scotland, the precious royal Regalia were used – the Scottish crown, the sceptre, and the sword. After Charles's defeat at Worcester, Cromwell's troops in the north set about subduing Scotland as well. The Regalia were spirited away to Dunnottar by a minister's wife, who rode all the way along the coast, dressed as a peasant-woman. The Earl Marischal was then captured. The English, now knowing where the Regalia were, laid siege to Dunnottar. The Scottish Parliament sent in messages, begging its commander to smuggle out the Regalia, so that they could be taken elsewhere for safety. He refused to do so. He did send out, however, 176 valuable state documents, stitched into the corsets of his wife's cousin, Anne Lindsay, who walked right through the English lines unmolested. The siege went on for eight months, and the garrison surrendered only after ten days of continous artillery bombardment. The English rushed in and took the place apart. The Regalia were not there!

Some time before, they had been lowered on a string down to the shore on the seaward side of the Castle, where a serving-girl from the nearby manse of Kinneff scooped them into the basket in which she was collecting seaweed. They remained hidden under the floorboards of Kinneff Church until the Restoration. After the Union of Parliaments in 1707, they vanished again. Some people thought they were in England. In 1818, as the result of a hunch by Sir Walter Scott, the Regalia turned up in a locked chest in a barred room in Edinburgh Castle, into which no one had been for 111 years. They are in the Castle still, but now for everyone to see!

Poets and Story-tellers
The earliest surviving fragment of Scottish poetry begins: 'When Alysandyr our King was dede / That Scotland led in luve and le ...' (When Alexander our King was dead, who

led Scotland in love and peace ...). It was written shortly after the death of Alexander III in 1286, and mourns the passing of arguably the best king the country ever had. Not all Scottish verse is on such a lofty theme. Another piece, written before 1500, celebrates ironically the pleasures of football, among them, as still today, 'Brissit brawnis and broken banis / Strife, discord and wastit wanis ... ' (Torn muscles and cracked bones, / Strife, dissent and broken homes ...).

The language in which the people of the Lowlands wrote in medieval times is called Middle Scots. After James VI (himself no mean poet) transferred the royal court to London, English became the polite language of Scottish poetry, though the composers and singers of ballads retained a fair element of Scots as well as traditional Scottish themes (violence, battle, romance – mainly of the tragic kind –, and the supernatural) in that unique and splendid body of national verse. In the eighteenth century Scots resurfaced as a medium of poetry, notably in the hands of the incomparable Burns, but the great nineteenth-century novelists, Scott, Galt, and Stevenson, employed it only in the speech of the lower classes. Though English had been the official language of Scotland since the 1707 Act of Union, there was a political as well as a cultural reaction against it in the 1920s, spearheaded by the poet Hugh MacDiarmid (1892-1978), and continued by William Soutar (1898-1943), Sydney Goodsir Smith (1915-75), Robert Garioch (1909-81), Maurice Lindsay (b. 1918), and others.

Gaelic poetry belongs to a completely different tradition, with its roots in the bardic songs and tales. Because Gaelic itself is a separate language, its literature has developed independently of that in Scots or English. Alexander Carmichael (1832-1912) spent most of his life, when not working as a civil servant, recording and translating Gaelic oral material into English, which was published in five volumes as *Carmina Gadelica*. Such was the oral tradition that the first contemporary book of Gaelic poetry did not appear until 1751, and Duncan Ban McIntyre (1724-1812) could not write at all, and had to have his published works written out for him. Duncan Ban sang with huge gusto about anything that appealed to him, especially deer-hunting and drinking. Where Duncan Ban's poetry celebrates the raw landscape and the mountain slopes, the best-known poem of Alexander Macdonald (c.1700-80), *The Birlinn of Clanranald*, is all about a sea-voyage, told with exactness and an eye to every detail. Ironically, the most influential eighteenth-century work of Gaelic literature was largely a fraud. James Macpherson (1736-96) went into the Highlands in search of a lost epic poem about the third-century hero Fingal, supposed to have been composed by his son Ossian. It is probable that on his travels Macpherson did hear some genuine fragments, but his translation of the whole epic of Fingal, published in 1761, contains much of his own creation. Today, there are more than twenty publishers of books in Gaelic, maintaining the literature as well as the language. Nor is the tradition any longer so isolated, in that two of Scotland's most eminent contemporary poets, Derick Thomson (b. 1921) and Iain Crichton Smith (b. 1928), who is also a novelist, are bilingual, and write with equal facility in either language.

Women, no less than men, have featured as writers in all three languages. One of the most heart-breaking of all Scottish love lyrics, written in Gaelic by Isabel Stewart, Countess of Argyll (d. 1510), describes the anguish of a mistress on her lover's death, all the more intense because she cannot share it with anyone. Mary MacLeod (1569-1674) was nurse, and unofficial bard, to the chief of the Macleods at Dunvegan Castle, Skye, though at one point she was banished to another island, from which she sent at least one poem begging for return. She lived to an enormous age, apparently bibulous to the last. Another female Gaelic bard was Mary Macpherson (1821-98), whose energy, presence, and outspokenness against oppression and injustice, were alike of heroic proportions. Another genuine heroine was Lady Grisell Baillie (1665-1746). At the age of twelve, she was the secret messenger between her father, a fervent supporter of the Covenant, and the man whose son she ultimately married, who was awaiting execution in Edinburgh Castle. She then hid her father from the Government troops and, after his escape to Holland, got the whole family there, an operation that involved carrying a sick sister for twenty miles on foot through the muddy countryside. In her reworking in Scots of traditional songs, she was followed by a number of equally talented ladies. They included Jean Elliot (1727-1805), whose 'The Flowers of the Forest' recalls the tragedy of Flodden; Lady Anne Barnard (1750-1825), author of the touching 'Auld Robin Gray'; Lady Nairne (1766-1845), among whose Jacobite songs are 'Will ye no' come back again?' and 'The Hundred Pipers', and who also wrote 'The Land of the Leal' and the echoing song of the street-cries, 'Caller Herrin'; and Lady Scott (1810-1900), another Jacobite songstress, but better known for her version of 'Annie Laurie', albeit rather inferior to the original one by William Douglas of Fingland, written in about 1690. Marion Angus (1866-1946) lived all her life in or near Aberdeen, and did not publish a book of poetry until she was fifty-six. She wrote with great assurance in both Scots and English, in which her most accomplished poem is her lament for Mary, Queen of Scots, 'Alas, Poor Queen'. Violet Jacob (1863-1946) came from the northeast, too, and wrote poetry in the dialect of that region. She also wrote historical novels. In a way, more original than any of these, because each speaks entirely with her own voice, are Liz Lochhead (b. 1947) and Valerie Gillies (b. 1948).

The first two novels about contemporary Highland life were written by women – *The Cottages of Glenburnie* (1808) by Elizabeth Hamilton (1758-1816), and *Discipline* (1814) by Mary Brunton (1778-1818). The novel of social observation and manners was such a new genre, however, that the first two novels by Susan Ferrier (1782-1854), *Marriage* and *Inheritance*, were, at her own request, published anonymously. If she has, rightly, been compared with Jane Austen, then Margaret Oliphant (1828-97) may be regarded as the Scottish answer to Anthony Trollope. She wrote over a hundred best-selling novels of English and Scottish provincial life, and twenty-eight historical and biographical works, besides innumerable articles. Equally prolific was Annie S. Swan (1859-1943), who began by writing in the vein of Mrs Oliphant, but found an even more profitable market for light romantic fiction. As talented and versatile as any was Elizabeth Mackintosh (1897-1952), a former PT instructor, who wrote biographies and historical drama as Gordon Daviot, and detective mysteries as Josephine Tey. Muriel Spark (b. 1918) was born and educated in Edinburgh, which inspired her sixth and most famous novel, *The Prime of Miss Jean Brodie*. The novelist and short story writer Elspeth Davie (b. 1919) was born in Ayrshire, but most of her work has a background of contemporary Edinburgh.

As remarkable as any of these women writers, and the youngest subject in the *Dictionary of National Biography*, was Marjory Fleming, who died in Kirkcaldy in 1811 from measles at the age of eight, having written, under the eye of her personal tutor, her older cousin Isabella Keith, three manuscript books containing nine thousand words of prose in journal form and 560 lines of verse. Some of her work was published in 1858, and a complete edition in 1934. Its acute observation, as well as its natural freshness, give it lasting charm.

The earliest-known Scottish poet is John Barbour (c.1320-95), Archdeacon of Aberdeen and author of *The Bruce*, a long, patriotic rhyming poem about Robert I's fight to free Scotland from English domination. It is remarkable for its detail, for its accuracy, and for the poet's attention also to the common people who helped to make their King's dream a reality. James I did not waste his captivity in England, where he had a good education and spent much of the time at court, an experience which is reflected in the allegorical poem he wrote for his English bride, *The Kingis Quair* (The King's Book), certainly the finest poem ever written by a reigning monarch. James IV inherited his great-grandfather's taste for poetry, and his court was the scene of comings and goings of poets. One of these was 'Blind Harry', though whether he was actually blind, and whether Harry was his real name, we are not sure. Whoever he was, he had an eye for the market. His lengthy historical romance in verse, *Sir William Wallace*, is violently anti-English, and its hero is a lusty fighter and ladies' man, whose escapades are a series of cliffhangers, liberally sprinkled with graphic descriptions of battle and gore.

It was the age of the Scottish Renaissance. The poet Robert Henryson (d.c. 1490), probably a lawyer and possibly a cleric, was writing his fables, lightly based on Aesop, but crammed with wit and insight, and featuring animals described with the same attention to detail as Beatrix Potter gave her creations five hundred years later. His *Testament of Cresseid* is the Troilus and Cressida tragedy, told from the point at which, having left Troilus for Diomede, Cressida is in turn deserted by her new lover, and is then struck with leprosy. As she sits by the roadside with her leper's cup and clapper, Troilus rides by. Something reminds him of the girl he once knew, but they do not recognise each other. Gavin Douglas (c.1474-1522), the same who after James IV's death contested the archbishopric of St Andrews, was engaged in his translation into 'Scottis meter' of Virgil's *Aeneid*. The

argumentative and melancholy William Dunbar (c. 1460-c. 1521) was much at court, writing satirical poems, religious poems, love poems, moral poems and poems of admonition to the King, always hoping for a church living, and frequently complaining about his pension. Also there was Sir David Lyndsay of the Mount, tutor to the King's heir, James V, and later Lyon King of Arms. He was an accomplished poet, and his moral drama, *Ane Satyr of the Three Estaitis*, performed at Linlithgow Palace in 1540, makes him the first known Scottish playwright.

The second great age of Scottish poetry effectively began with Allan Ramsay (1684-1758), an Edinburgh wig-maker who was an adept writer of lightish verse. More importantly, by publishing collections of traditional poetry, and by turning his shop into the first Scottish circulating library and a haunt for like-minded citizens, he put Scotland back on the British literary map, from which it had disappeared after the transfer of the court to London in 1603 and of the Government in 1707. In the atmosphere Ramsay established, Robert Fergusson (1750-74) was able to experiment not so much with a true Scots, but with a composite, poetic language, using words from different dialects. Fergusson died in a mad-house when he was just twenty-four. He was a much better poet in Scots than he was in English, and he had done enough to inspire the man who became Scotland's national poet.

The greatness of Robert Burns (1759-96) has not been overestimated. He is one of the few major poets in any language to have overcome the handicap of an indigent upbringing and rudimentary education. He was an outspoken critic of hypocrisy and a champion of the rights of the poor. He struggled all his life with poverty, and he died of rheumatic fever at the age of thirty-seven. He is a poet of simple concepts, simply expressed, and he wrote equally well in Scots and English, sometimes using both in the same poem. His output and range were prodigious, but it is for his love songs, his nature poems, and his scary folktale *Tam o' Shanter*, that he is best known and remembered the world over, especially on his birthday.

James Hogg (1770-1835), known as the 'Ettrick Shepherd', lacked a formal education, but he made up for it by imbibing deeply Border folklore and ballads. He really was a shepherd, but latterly his journalism, novels, short stories and poetry proved more profitable than his agricultural ventures. John Galt (1779-1839) was a businessman and novelist whose acute perception makes his works valuable sources of information about social, political and religious issues of the times. The literary giant of the day was Sir Walter Scott (1771-1832), true founder of the genre of the historical novel and still its most famous exponent. His interest in Scottish history, and in presenting it fairly, was matched by his vigilance in recovering and publishing Scotland's heritage of folklore and ballads, and he also wrote many fine ballad-epics of his own. He was plagued all his life by crippling pains and illness. When the publishing and printing businesses with which he was associated failed in the slump of the 1820s he, too, was declared bankrupt, but he still regarded himself as responsible for the firms' liabilities. He refused the help of friends, of whom he had many, declaring of his debts: 'This right hand shall work them all off.' All the debts were finally settled, but the effort of writing non-stop for six years killed him.

Ill-health also dogged the much shorter life of Robert Louis Stevenson (1850-94), author of *Treasure Island, Kidnapped*, and *The Strange Case of Dr Jekyll and Mr Hyde*. He was also a master of the short story, whose tales of supernatural possession, *Thrawn Janet* and *Markheim* in particular, and the uncompleted novel *The Weir of Hermiston*, are additionally important for what they tell us about Scotland and the Scots. Sir J.M. Barrie (1860-1937) was a writer of a very different kind, whose early works presented a much cosier picture of Scottish rural life, and gave him the dubious distinction of being the first member of what came pejoratively to be known as the 'Kailyard' school of novelists. He was also the first major Scottish-born dramatist, whose *Peter Pan* is perennially and hugely popular. The reputation of John Buchan (1875-1940) as the author of *The Thirty-Nine Steps* and the creator of Richard Hannay tends to obscure the fact that he was a notable literary figure and statesman who, as Lord Tweedsmuir, was Governor-General of Canada 1935-40. Other twentieth-century novelists who, each in his own fashion, illuminated the Scottish way of life are Sir Compton Mackenzie (1883-1974), Neil M. Gunn (1891-1973), George Blake (1893-1961), Eric Linklater (1899-1974), and Lewis Grassic Gibbon (1901-35). George Mackay Brown (b. 1921) writes as vividly as any of these in reflecting the origins, history, folklore, communal and religious life, and the sea-girt, rugged landscape of his native Orkney, while demonstrating the Scottish talent for versatility, since he excels as a poet and a short story writer, as well as a novelist.

Doctors and Scientists

In 1506, James IV granted royal recognition to the Guild of Surgeons and Barbers in Edinburgh, which had been established the previous year. In 1567, the surgeons and apothecaries combined as one body, whose members then ceased to act as barbers. A royal charter was obtained from George III in 1778, when they became the Royal College of Surgeons of the City of Edinburgh. The Royal College of Physicians of Edinburgh was founded in 1617.

Glasgow was slower to recognise its medical profession, perhaps because the western Scot was more reluctant to part with his money for services of doubtful efficacy. Just as, in the remoter parts of the Highlands at the beginning of the twentieth century, medical treatment consisted of tar for the sheep and whisky for the people, so the sixteenth-century Glaswegian preferred to bathe an injured part in the Molendinar Burn than go to the doctor. Even so, the Royal Faculty of Physicians and Surgeons of Glasgow was established in 1635, and thereafter the City Council took a paternal interest in their medical suppliers, decreeing, for instance, in August 1685 that the treasurer pay the surgeon John Hall forty pounds Scots for curing one James Hamilton of a 'white scabbed head'. Some suspicion of doctors continued, however. In the early eighteenth century a Dr Campbell is said to have invented a gastroscope, for internal examination of the stomach. Looking for a volunteer on whom to experiment, he went to the Glasgow Fair and approached a sword-swallower, who refused with the words, 'I know I can swallow a sword, but I'll be damned if I can swallow a trumpet.'

Early medical science was closely allied to botany. Edinburgh had the first public botanical garden, established in 1661 when the governors of Heriot's Hospital (the school for orphans established under the will of George Heriot, jeweller and banker to James VI) instructed their gardener to lay out a medicinal herb garden, which would be open to anyone who wanted to study the plants. The distinguished physicians Sir Andrew Balfour (1630-94) and Sir Robert Sibbald (1641-1722), Physician to the King, Geographer Royal, President of the Royal Society of Physicians, and first Professor of Medicine at the University of Edinburgh, had more ambitious plans. First, they set up their garden (forty feet square) in the grounds of Holyroodhouse and bullied their colleagues into contributing to its upkeep and to the importation of foreign plants. They then got the lease of a larger site at the east end of the Nor' Loch – a plaque on the wall in Waverley Station marks the spot. There was a setback in 1689, at the time of the famous exit from Parliament of Graham of Claverhouse. The supporters of William and Mary who were besieging the Castle, still held in the name of James VII, decided to drain the Nor' Loch. This inundated the botanical garden which, when the water was later drawn off, was found to be covered with a thick deposit of mud. Many delicate plants were destroyed, but the keeper, James Sutherland, and his staff did such good work in repairing the damage that he was awarded a pension by the Privy Council. The garden remained there for another ninety years before being transferred to Leith Walk, and then, in 1894, to its present site in Inverleith Row. Another distinguished Scottish physician/botanist was William Wells (1757-1817) who, in 1814, gave the first exact explanation of the nature of dew.

Scottish medicine has fostered some notable families, none more so than the Monro father, son and grandson, each called Alexander, who successively held the chair of anatomy at the University of Edinburgh from 1720 to 1846. The first of them had made an unusual bargain with the Town Council, that if they undertook to appoint his son as his successor, he would give him the best training possible at home and abroad. The third Professor Monro was inhibited by his predecessors and handicapped by the rivalry of the impressive Dr John Barclay (1758-1826). Barclay was lecturing one day on anatomy, with a table in front of him covered by a sheet. At the climax of his discourse he whipped away the sheet to give a practical demonstration. There was nothing underneath it: someone had forgotten to supply the corpse. Barclay carried on, quite unabashed. William Hunter (1718-83) was a surgeon turned physician – he was fined £1 by the Surgeons' Corporation of London for joining the Royal College of Physicians without asking their permission –, and became the founder of the modern science of gynaecology. The Hunterian Museum and Art Gallery of the University of Glasgow are named after him. William fell out with his brother John (1728-93) over which of them was responsible for certain anatomical discoveries, but John went on to become surgeon extraordinary to George III, surgeon-general of the army, and innovator of many aspects of scientific surgery. The Bells were another Scottish medical family. Sir Charles Bell (1774-1842) is regarded as the founder of neurology, after whom the affliction Bell's Palsy is named. His brother John (1763-1820) was a noted Edinburgh surgeon who commanded large fees for his services. A laird once sent a cheque for £50, which Bell regarded as rather less than he deserved. He went and called on his patient and, when the butler opened the door, tossed the cheque at him, saying, 'You have gone to considerable trouble opening the door for me, so here is a trifle for you.' The laird took the hint. A relative of theirs, Dr Joseph Bell (1837-1911), was the model for Arthur Conan Doyle's Sherlock Holmes.

William Hunter had been a private pupil in Hamilton of William Cullen (1710-1790), who compiled the first complete medical guide, and invented a mechanical ice-making machine. Hunter later lodged with another Scottish surgeon and a friend of Cullen, Dr William Smellie (1697-1763), who practised as a man-midwife, and was a pioneer of obstetrics, using for his teaching a model made by himself of real bones covered with leather. Cullen later became Professor of Anatomy and Chemistry at the University of Glasgow, where one of his pupils was Joseph Black (1728-99), a scientist of such gifts that after he had been appointed to succeed his teacher, he decided to switch jobs with the Professor of Medicine. While continuing to teach, Black found the time also to do astonishing work in physics as well as chemistry, including the discovery of latent heat and of the formation of carbon dioxide.

In 1814, there were eight hundred students of anatomy in Glasgow but no shortage of bodies on which to practise, though the only legal way of obtaining them was by permission of relatives (rarely given) or by using victims of the gallows. Indeed, there is a reliable report that the supply was better, and cheaper, than in Edinburgh, and that corpses were regularly transferred there from Glasgow to meet the demand. Until the Anatomy Act of 1832, body-snatchers plied their ghastly trade in both cities, but the Edinburgh doss-house keepers Burke and Hare ran a more labour intensive operation. They murdered their lodgers and sold the bodies to an anatomy lecturer and fellow of the Edinburgh College of Surgeons, Robert Knox (1791-1862). Their secret was blown when students started to recognise some of the bodies. Burke was hanged in High Street. Hare saved himself by turning evidence, but was hounded out of Scotland and ended his life as a blind beggar in London. Dr Knox continued his career as a respected lecturer.

It is said that even the most famous of all Scottish surgeons, Robert Liston (1794-1847), was as a student involved in several body-snatching escapades. His early training bore fruit, however. He was the first surgeon to remove a shoulder-blade, and his skill and strength were such that even before anaesthetics he could amputate a leg at the thigh with only a single assistant to hold the limb steady. One of Liston's pupils, and his successor as the pre-

eminent surgeon in Scotland, was James Syme (1799-1870), who was a pioneer of plastic surgery and of amputation at the ankle-joint, and the first to realise the importance of leaving a wound open until the blood stopped oozing. Syme's surgical assistant from 1853 to 1856 was an Englishman, Joseph (later Baron) Lister (1827-1912), who married Syme's daughter, became Professor of Surgery at Glasgow and of Clinical Surgery at Edinburgh, and was the founder of antiseptic surgery. Sir William Macewen (1848-1924) was the first of the modern brain surgeons, and introduced the operation for mastoid.

The pioneer of anaesthesia was Sir James Young Simpson (1811-70), an Edinburgh baker's son who was appointed Professor of Midwifery at the University of Edinburgh when he was twenty-eight. Determined to find a really satisfactory way of removing pain from an operation, he experimented in 1847 on himself and two assistants with chloroform, which was then used only as a solvent – all three of them ended up under the table, insensible. A fortnight, later, a boy was successfully operated on in the Royal Infirmary for the removal of a diseased bone from his arm, having been given chloroform by Simpson. And in the same year, he presided at the birth of the first baby to be delivered alive by anaesthesia – her name was Wilhelmina Carstairs. Nevertheless, there was opposition to anaesthetics until Queen Victoria, to whom Simpson was physician in Scotland, was given chloroform while giving birth to Prince Leopold in 1853. Sir James was the first doctor practising in Scotland to become a baronet.

The list of other Scottish doctors who have by their skill and dedicated research alleviated pain and found cures for diseases is long and distinguished. It includes Robert Whytt (1714-66), who first propounded the theory of the source of involuntary movement and of hysteria as a cause of illness; James Lind (1716-94), who found the answer to scurvy and devised a method for making fresh water at sea; Alexander Stewart (1813-83), who distinguished between typhoid and typhus, and successfully treated both; Sir Patrick Manson (1844-1922) and Sir Ronald Ross (1857-1939), the pioneers of tropical medicine, who between them discovered the cause of malaria; Sir Robert Philip (1857-1939), who set up the world's first tuberculosis clinic in Edinburgh: Sir Robert Muir (1864-1959), pioneer of immunology; Sir William Boog Leishman (1865-1926), the first to perfect a typhoid vaccine; and Sir Alexander Fleming (1881-1955), the Ayrshire farmer's boy who discovered penicillin.

The Scottish talent for invention is nowhere more evident than in our daily lives. Charles Mackintosh (1766-1843) followed up a suggestion by Professor James Syme and produced the first waterproof cloth, as well as the coat that bears his name. James Chalmers (1782-1853) devised the adhesive postage stamp, and Alexander Bain (1810-77) the electric clock. Kirkpatrick Macmillan (1813-78), a Dumfriesshire blacksmith, built the first pedal bicycle with front-wheel steering, and rode it to Glasgow, a journey which took him two painful days. The pain was taken out of cycling, and other travel by road, by John Boyd Dunlop (1840-1921), who invented the pneumatic tyre, not knowing that a prototype had been made fifty years earlier by another Scot, Robert Thomson (1822-1873), but abandoned because of the price of rubber – a more permanent invention of Thomson was the fountain pen. The Dunlop tyre made possible the development not only of the motor car but also of the aeroplane. The airport 'tarmac' is a version of another Scottish invention, the road surface made by John Macadam (1756-1836), and planes are guided in and out by radar, the wartime brainchild of Sir Robert Watson Watt (1892-1973). Sir James Dewar (1842-1923) produced the first vacuum flask, and Alexander Graham Bell (1847-1922) the telephone. Credit for making the first television transmission goes to John Logie Baird (1888-1946), an enigmatic genius whose contribution during the Second World War is so secret that even his family still cannot be told what it comprised.

Still considered one of the most impressive Scottish men of learning is the mathematician John Napier of Merchiston (1550-1617), inventor of logarithms, of the earliest calculating machine ('Napier's Bones'), and of the notation for decimal fractions used today. He also designed an armoured tank and a submarine. Surprisingly for a man of science, he was also a believer in astrology and divination, and was said to have a jet-black cock as his familiar. The Napier College of advanced education is built on the site of his Edinburgh home and incorporates in its design the fifteenth-century tower in which he lived.

The other great Scottish mechanical wizard was James Watt (1736-1819). He did not actually invent the steam engine, but it was while repairing a model of an earlier and rather inefficient engine devised by Thomas Newcomen that, walking on Glasgow Green one Sunday afternoon in the spring of 1765, Watt hit on the idea of the separate container, or condenser, which utterly revolutionised the manufacturing, engineering and transport industries, and led to the Industrial Revolution. He did invent the double-acting engine, however, and a host of other items associated with the development and use of his own engine, in the course of which he coined the word 'horsepower'. He went into partnership in Birmingham with the engineer Matthew Boulton. In 1778 Boulton took on to their staff a young man called William Murdoch (1754-1839), who had walked all the way from his home village of Auchinleck in Ayrshire to seek a job. While still employed by the firm of Boulton and Watt, Murdoch devised and successfully demonstrated his system of gas lighting. Neither partner was very impressed, and thus the firm lost the chance to take out a patent for it, and Murdoch, who never showed any bitterness, the opportunity to benefit financially from his invention.

The first man to put a Watt steam engine in a ship was William Symington (1763-1831), and the world's first steamship, owned by Patrick Miller (1773-1825), chugged sedately across Dalswinton Loch in 1788. Public tranport by steamship was another Scottish 'first'. In 1812, Henry Bell's *Comet* began sailing between places on the Clyde, and even ventured as far as Fort William, via the Crinan Canal. The man who put the engine in the *Comet* was David Napier (1790-1869), who later invented the steeple-engine and designed the revolutionary ship's hull that tapered to a point at the bows.

The memorials of the great Scottish civil engineers of the eighteenth and nineteenth centuries are modern wonders still. The suspension bridge over the Menai Straits in Wales, the Gota Canal in Sweden, the Caledonian Canal and the rebuilt Crinan Canal, as well as Edinburgh's soaring Dean Bridge, are the work of Thomas Telford (1757-1834), a shepherd's son from the Borders. The five-arch bridge which crosses the Tweed at Kelso, the first with an elliptic arch, was built by John Rennie (1761-1821), who used a similar design for the old Waterloo Bridge in London, which lasted until the 1930s. Sir William Arrol (1839-1913), who started his working life as a blacksmith, built the railway bridges over the Forth and the Tay, and the El Giza bridge across the Nile at Cairo, and designed the steelwork of London Bridge. The Bell Rock lighthouse, on a dangerous reef off Arbroath, was the work of Robert Stevenson (1772-1850), one of a family of distinguished lighthouse engineers and the grandfather of Robert Louis Stevenson.

Scottish physicists have excelled in various fields of discovery. Sir John Leslie (1766-1832) was the first person to freeze water by the use of an air pump, and invented a differential thermometer, a hygrometer, and a photometer (for measuring light). William Thomson, later Lord Kelvin (1824-1907), appointed Professor of Natural Philosophy at Glasgow when he was twenty-two, propounded the second law of thermodynamics, constructed many devices for measuring energy, laid the foundations for the development of refrigeration and radio-communication, and supervised the laying of the first transatlantic telegraph cable. James Clerk Maxwell (1831-79), became the first Professor of Experimental Physics at Cambridge University, where he supervised the building and organised the first work of the Cavendish Laboratory. He was a founder of the study of electronics and of statistical mechanics, and proposed many new theories about the nature of light and gases. He also devised the first colour photograph.

It is perhaps a measure of a strict Calvinist upbringing and of the discipline of the old Scottish brand of education, imposed upon a closely-knit society in which class barriers have traditionally had little meaning, that so many Scottish doctors and scientists have been able to harness creative thought to dedicated research, and to achieve international distinction often from humble beginnings. Humble beginnings, too, heralded one of Scotland's most widely-enjoyed culinary inventions. Henry VIII is recorded as being delighted to receive in 1524 the gift of 'a box of Marmalade', which consisted of preserved quinces – *marmelo* is Portuguese for 'quince'. Among all kinds of produce landed at the port of Dundee in the early 1700s were oranges from Seville, which were so bitter that no one would buy them. An enterprising family called Keiller bought them up and made a jam from them, which they sold from their grocer's shop as a preserve. The response was such that in 1792 the then owner of the business, James Keiller, set up the world's first marmalade factory, using his mother's recipe.

The Scot Abroad

The Scots introduced golf to America and Japan, peaches to New South Wales, Presbyterianism to India and New Zealand, printing to Uganda, and curling to just about everywhere that the game is played. There are seven Aberdeens in the USA, and one each in Australia, South Africa, Hong Kong and Canada. There is a New Glasgow in Nova Scotia, Canada, too, which itself is an even earlier example of Scottish influence overseas.

When the European nations parcelled out the Americas among themselves at the beginning of the seventeenth century, by laying extravagant claims, like Spain and Portugal, or by founding settlements, as did England, France, Holland and Sweden, the Scots saw no reason to be left out of the act. Indeed, James VI, who had already given his name to Jamestown, Virginia, the English settlement capital, was keen that there should also be a Scottish presence in North America. In 1621, Sir William Alexander, later Earl of Stirling, acting on the recommendation of the English Governor of Newfoundland, where there were a number of Scots working the plantations, got from James the grant of the territory of 'Nova Scotia in America', thus emulating New England, New France, and New Netherlands.

To generate interest in Scotland's first colony, and to get settlers and money, Alexander, with the King's assent, proposed that baronetcies should be conferred on any who would contribute six men and a thousand merks. It was not even necessary for the new baronets to go to Novia Scotia to claim their 'estates'. A portion of what is now the Esplanade of Edinburgh Castle was designated Nova Scotian territory, and here they solemnly took possession of their symbolic pieces of ground. The scheme lapsed, and Nova Scotia was in any case surrendered in 1632 to the French, in whose hands it remained until 1713, but the baronetcies are still in force. Alexander's birthplace, Menstrie Castle, has recently been restored, and the coats of arms of all 109 baronets are there on permanent display.

The specific Glasgow connection with Nova Scotia came about in 1819, when a party of distressed weavers from the west of Scotland, who were having a particularly hard time in the wake of mechanisation, founded New Glasgow, which, by the end of the century had, like its namesake, become the centre of a thriving shipbuilding industry. When Canada became a dominion in 1867, Nova Scotia was one of its original states. The creator of the Dominion of Canada, and its first Prime Minister, was John A. Macdonald (1815-95), who was born in Glasgow and emigrated with his family from Sutherland in 1820. The only satisfactory way of uniting British Columbia on the west coast with the states in the east, and of linking all of them with the central prairies, lakes and mountainous districts, was to build a railway right across the country. This was Macdonald's aim. It was a vast enterprise. The railway would be the world's longest and most expensive, covering two-and-a-half thousand miles of some of the most difficult territory in the world, much of it not yet explored, let alone mapped.

It was another Scot, Kirkcaldy-born Sandford Fleming (1827-1915), who proposed a workable plan for the Canadian Pacific Railway, and he became its first engineer-in-chief. To survey possible routes, he and a small party (which included a Scottish Presbyterian minister) travelled over five thousand miles in three months, often on foot. Two other Scottish-born immigrants, Donald A. Smith (1820-1914) and his cousin, George Stephen (1829-1921), founded the company which built the railway between 1871 and 1875, though several times they faced the collapse of the enterprise and personal ruin. The project was finally saved when the company undertook to transport three thousand troops halfway across the country in mid-winter to put down an Indian revolt. The operation succeeded, in spite of the fact that there were still four vast gaps in the line. When the last spike of the completed railway was hammered into the ground, a journey which had previously taken six months by ox-cart from coast to coast could now be made in six days.

To a migrant Scot, whether pulled by will or pushed by necessity, hardship was a secondary consideration, though the establishment of a Scottish settlement on the isthmus of Darien, now Panama, led to the greatest national disaster since the Battle of Flodden. The basic idea was brave, imaginative, and not unsound. It was proposed in 1695 by the Dumfriesshire-born financial genius, William Patterson (1653-1719), fresh from founding the Bank of England the previous year. European merchandise to and from India and other parts of Asia, instead of being sent round the Cape of Good Hope or the even more dangerous Cape Horn, could be unloaded on one side of the isthmus, carried across, and shipped again from the port on the other side. After English participation in the scheme was scotched by King William and the English Parliament, egged on by the English East India Company, the notion of a genuine Scottish colony, 'New Caledonia', caught on in Scotland, and the necessary money was raised. In 1699, three separate expeditions, with two-and-a-half thousand emigrants, sailed for Darien. Only a few survived, one of whom was a shattered William Patterson. The last settlers were ejected by Spanish troops, but whether the real villain of the piece was King William or the malarial mosquito has been argued ever since.

During the seventeenth century, however, more Scots went to North America as prisoners than genuine emigrants. These included prisoners-of-war, captured at the battles of Preston, Dunbar and Worcester during the Civil War, and Covenanters – one ship, carrying two hundred victims of the defeat at Bothwell Brig, went down off Orkney in 1679, with no survivors. And even more people, perhaps a tenth of the whole population of Scotland, went to Ireland or to Europe (many initially as mercenaries) to evade the failing Scottish economy and the growing discipline of the Reformed Church.

The second great wave of emigration to North America, which reached its peak in the 1770s, was largely a voluntary one. When the role of the Highland tacksmen, who acted as controllers of land and properties on behalf of their chiefs, ceased largely to exist, many of them, rather than be downgraded, emigrated, often taking their tenants with them. Irresistible, too, to a people oppressed by the loss of their livelihood to the sheep farms, were the letters home from satisfied emigrants. James Boswell, who visited the Hebrides with Dr Johnson in 1773, describes a local dance called 'America': 'Each of the couples ... successively whirls round in a circle, till all are in motion; and the dance seems intended to show how emigration catches, till a whole neighbourhood is set afloat.' Of course, the journey itself, by sailing ship, and in awful conditions, would take nine weeks or more, and the hard work did not begin until the hopeful emigrants had actually disembarked. Then there was the trek, on foot or by ox-cart, to the chosen settlement, the building of a home with one's own hands, and the carving of an existence out of the land.

Perhaps the most extraordinary of such pilgrimages began in 1817, 'to the wail of the bagpipes and the singing of McCrimmon's Lament', as a shipload of evicted crofters set sail from Lochbroom in Skye, bound for Pictou in Nova Scotia. They landed after a very rough voyage, but two hundred of them decided to move on, and in 1820 embarked for the Ohio region, by a route which would take them up the Mississippi via the Gulf of Mexico. They had only gone a few miles when a storm blew them back into the harbour of St Ann's, where they decided they had had enough travel for the time being, and settled again. In 1847, however, the aspirations of many of them, including their leader, Rev. Norman MacLeod, turned to Australia. It took several years to build and provision the necessary transport, but in 1851 one ship reached Adelaide after 'a delightful voyage' of 164 days. Still not satisfied, they moved on to Melbourne, and then, in 1853, having sent out scouts by cutter, they finally made Auckland, New Zealand. Here they met up with the other shipload of their original companions, and formed the community still known as the Waipu Highlanders.

The earliest Scottish settlers in New Zealand, as in many parts of Africa, had been missionaries, closely followed by a growing number of farmers and other professional people. After the Disruption of 1843, when the Free Church broke away from the Church of Scotland, a strictly Free Church settlement was established in the Otago region, called Dunedin, rather than 'New Edinburgh', as had been proposed at first. By contrast, the first Scottish settlers in Australia were convicts or political martyrs, some of the latter of whom were allowed to set up their own farms. Scottish interest in Australia grew quickly, perhaps due to the fact that two Scots successively governed New South Wales from 1809 to 1825, Lachlan Macquarrie and Sir Thomas Brisbane, who also successfully combined the careers of soldier and astronomer. In 1839, two-thirds of the inhabitants of Melbourne were said to have been Scots. And between 1891 and 1921 there was recorded a consistent figure of a hundred thousand people in Australia who had been born in Scotland, compared with three hundred and fifty thousand born in England, which had a population about eight times that of Scotland.

Sir Walter Scott wrote in 1821 in a letter to his friend Lord Montagu, brother of the Duke of Buccleuch, that India 'is the corn chest for Scotland where we poor gentry must send our younger sons as we send our black cattle to the south'. Many of these younger sons did very well for themselves, however, and for India, none more so than Hon. Mountstuart Elphinstone (1779-1859), who arrived in India when he was sixteen. As Governor of Bombay 1819-27, he founded a system of administration which took into account eastern sensibilities as well as western attitudes. His influence on education was considerable as well. He had already established a Hindu college at Poona, and as President, during his governorship, of the Society for the Promotion of Education, he ensured that education would be fostered in the national languages. Elphinstone College in Bombay was founded as a mark of respect to him on his retirement, and two professorships were endowed by Indians of all religious faiths, who subscribed to the cost of £10,000. Less laudable was his habit of executing criminals by tying them to the muzzle of a howitzer and blowing them to pieces, which, he used to explain, had the essential elements of being 'painless to the criminal and terrible to the beholder'. It also ensured that there was no body with which the statutory religious rites could be performed.

Elphinstone's successor as governor was another Scottish younger son, Sir John Malcolm (1769-1833), who was a soldier of distinction and had been Britain's first ambassador to Persia since the reign of Elizabeth. Because of the failure of his father's speculations, Malcolm had been entered by an uncle for military service as an officer with the East India Company when he was twelve. The interview board, unwilling to grant a commission to someone so young, put to him: ' My little man, what would you do if you met the Sultan of Mysore?' 'I'd cut off his head,' replied the boy imperturbably. He was accepted on the spot. A memorable interview also marked the beginning of the military career of Sir Colin Campbell (1792-1863), later Baron Clyde. He was born Colin Macliver, the son a Glasgow carpenter. When his uncle, Colonel John Campbell, took him when he was fifteen to see the Duke of York, Commander-in-Chief of the Army, the Duke got it wrong. 'Aha,' he cried, 'another of the Campbell clan', and wrote down the boy's name as Campbell. And Campbell it remained for the rest of his life. He commanded the 'thin red line' of Highlanders which won the Battle of Balaclava during the Crimean War, and then, at the age of sixty-five, was despatched to put down the Indian Mutiny as commander-in-chief. His first act in India was to relieve Lucknow in 1857. Lucknow had in fact already been relieved once, by the Seaforth Highlanders under Sir Henry Havelock and Sir James Outram, a feat recorded in the poem 'The Pipes at Lucknow' (written, confusingly enough, by an American, John Greenleaf Whittier), with its climactic lines: 'Then up spake a Scottish maiden, / With her ear unto the ground: / "Dinna ye hear it? – dinna ye hear it? / The pipes of Havelock sound."' The problem was that Havelock and Outram, and their troops, were now themselves boxed in, too, by fifty thousand sepoys. There they remained, for a further six weeks, until Campbell, with fewer than five thousand troops, but with the veteran Sutherland Highlanders at their head, forced his way in, and successfully evacuated the whole garrison, with the women and children.

No administrator did more for modern India than Lord Dalhousie (1812-60), who was born at the family seat of Dalhousie Castle in Midlothian. A professional politican, he was appointed Governor-General in 1847, in which capacity he was instrumental in completing the Grand Trunk Road and building several hundred miles of further metalled highways, in constructing the Ganges Canal, and in planning and setting up four thousand miles of telegraph lines. He also established the Indian railway system, with its many ramifications and implications, not the least of which, as he himself had predicted, was the start of the breakdown of caste distinctions, in that the railway companies refused to operate separate carriages for people of different castes. The Indian railways meant work not only for Scottish factories, but also for Scottish engineers and bridge-builders, railway managers, supervisors, accountants and foremen. A photograph taken in 1934, almost a hundred years later, shows a group of twenty-six men from the two adjacent Clackmannanshire parishes of Dollar and Muckhart, all of whom were then working in various capacities for the Bengal and North Western Railway, and the Rohilkund and Kumaon Railway, which covered the two adjoining states.

The Scottish wanderlust was not invariably collective. The explorer Mungo Park (1771-1806), seventh child of a Borders crofter, was the first white man to see the River Niger. On a second expedition, with his companions reduced to ten by heat, rains and fever, he travelled down it for 1300 miles before they were set upon and killed by natives. David Livingstone (1813-73), most famous and energetic of all African explorers, started working in the mill at Blantyre when he was ten, but was able to train as a medical missionary. His bent, however, was for travel, and in 1852 he wrote from Africa to the London Missionary Society, announcing that he proposed to explore a trade route from coast to coast across the centre of the continent, and asking them to look after his family. Without waiting for a reply, he shipped his wife and children back to Britain, and set out. Four years later, he had travelled halfway across to the west coast, and then all the way back to Quilimane on the east coast, by canoe, ox-cart and on foot, a journey of six thousand miles, during which he discovered the Victoria Falls. His final expedition lasted for seven years and ended in his death. He thought he had found a river which might be the Nile, and wanted to discover its source. In fact, it was the Congo, but he never knew this for certain. It was still a Scot, though, who did make the first exploration of the Nile's source, for James Grant (1827-92) shared the command with John Speke of the 1860 expedition which established the exact point.

As intrepid as any of these African explorers was the Dundee factory girl Mary Slessor (1848-1915), who spent all her adult life as a missionary in Calabar, waging a campaign against superstition and witchcraft. 'Run, Ma, run' was the cry when her help was needed. On one occasion, two warring chiefs and their armed retainers argued with each other for a day and a night, while Mary sat at her knitting under a coloured umbrella, putting in a word whenever things threatened to get out of hand. An equally colourful figure was John Clunies Ross (d. 1854), a native of Shetland who became self-styled king of the Cocos Islands in the Indian Ocean. In partnership with an Englishman, Alexander Hare, who had with him a few runaway slaves, Ross took possession of this uninhabited group of islands and, after Hare got bored and retired to Singapore, developed it into a thriving community. When the islands were declared British territory in 1857, John's son, John George, was appointed governor. John George married a high-ranking girl from Malaya, had six sons, all of whom were educated in Scotland, and himself visited Scotland in a schooner which had been built in his own shipyard.

Per head of population, the Scots may be regarded as the most widely dispersed nation in the world, as the existence of myriad Caledonian, Burns and clan societies demonstrates. Wherever they have gone, they have taken with them aspects of the different cultures and traditions which are the heritage of the modern Scot, and which echo the astonishing variety and contrasts of the Scottish landscape.

Facing page: autumn in the Highlands.

The standing stones of Scotland are one of the most awe-inspiring and evocative features of the people's heritage. No one knows their exact purpose, but they were most likely to have been social and religious centres associated with the worship of the spirit world. By the Loch of Stenness, Orkney, are the remains of two vast stone circles, about 5,000 years old. Facing page: the Ring of Brodgar, thirty-six of whose fifteen-foot-high stones survive out of the original sixty. Above: the three remaining stones of the Circle of Stenness, surrounded originally by a ditch, which it is estimated took 20,000 man hours to hew out of the solid rock.

Facing page: (top) the lower part of the circular Iron Age Broch of Gurness, Orkney, standing behind an array of stone huts which date from the subsequent Pictish and Viking ages, and (bottom) the rock formation at Yesnaby, Orkney. Top: part of the underground village complex at Skara Brae, Orkney, built in about 3000 B.C. Above: Marwick Head, Orkney, and the tower commemorating the sinking by a mine in 1916 of H.M.S. *Hampshire*, and the drowning of Lord Kitchener, Secretary of State for War, and most of the crew. The ship was taking him from Scapa Flow to Russia, and the circumstances of the disaster are still a mystery.

Centre left: Muckle Flugga, Shetland, the northernmost point of Scotland and (above left) fishing boats at Brae which reflect the islanders' dependence on the sea for their living. Facing page: the rugged cliffs of Esha Ness, on the west coast of the mainland of Shetland. Remaining pictures: Shetlanders celebrate their Viking origins in Lerwick at the annual fire festival of Up-Helly-A. An imitation Viking longship, with a raven banner at its masthead, is dragged through the town, accompanied by 'guisers' in Viking dress. Flaming torches are then flung into the ship and, as it burns, all sing the 'Lerwick Galley Song'.

At Sumburgh Head, Shetland, is the remarkable archaeological site of Jarlshof (top), comprising village settlements from the Bronze Age to Viking times, and a medieval farmhouse. Above: Esha Ness on a calm day. Facing page top: the harbour of Scalloway, west of Lerwick. The castle, which dates from 1600, was built by Earl Patrick Stewart – it was said that blood was mixed with mortar to reflect his cruelty to the people. He was himself executed in 1615, after which the castle fell into disuse. Facing page bottom: remains of the old fishing village of Stenness, Esha Ness.

Facing page top: Tiree, called by St Columba 'Land of Corn', has latterly depended on small-scale farming, reflected by this reconstructed traditional croft, with stones to keep the thatch in place. Facing page bottom: the cathedral and monastery of Iona, founded by St Columba, and the island of Mull behind. Top: Balephuil Bay, Tiree, and (left) Iona, from which Christianity spread to the rest of Scotland, and which was the burial place of early Scottish kings. The island itself is only three-and-a-half-miles long and one-and-half-miles wide. Fingal's Cave (above), in the uninhabited island of Staffa, off Mull, with its huge, black pillars of volcanic rock, was the inspiration for Mendelssohn's *Hebrides Overture*.

These pages: Balmoral Castle on Royal Deeside in Aberdeenshire. The original castle was leased to Queen Victoria in 1848, and bought by her husband in 1852, the climate being suggested by the royal doctor as the best for sufferers of rheumatism. A new, bigger castle was then built, a hundred yards away, by an Aberdeen architect under the supervision of Prince Albert and, when it was ready in 1855, the old one was razed. So, 252 years after James I had left Scotland for London, his great-great-great-great-great-great-granddaughter and her husband (who was also descended from James's daughter Elizabeth) had a permanent, and spectacular, Scottish home.

White Corries (top), near Glen Coe, is 2100 feet high, and served by a chair lift. Above: looming over the Pass of Glen Coe, the Three Sisters of Glen Coe, the lower peaks of the great Bidean nam Bian mountain. Facing page: a modern piper in full Highland uniform – with his sporran made of horsehair for military dress, and his *sgian dubh* in the right stocking – playing a lament at the actual site of the Massacre of Glencoe. The elemental magic and mystery of the Highlands can be seen and felt at the Falls of the River Coe (overleaf).

Above: the monument recording the massacre of the Macdonalds of Glen Coe by Government troops on 13 February 1692. Top, left and above left: the Pass of Glen Coe. Facing page: Loch Leven, whose bridge, carrying traffic between Fort William and Crianlarich, was opened in 1975. This particular Loch Leven is not to be confused with the other loch of the same name in Kinross-shire, where Mary, Queen of Scots was imprisoned. Overleaf: rhododendrons, especially rife in Scotland in June, form a foreground to Loch Leven.

Bonnie Prince Charlie first set foot on Scottish soil on 23 July 1745, on the island of Eriskay, Outer Hebrides. Early in August, he landed on the mainland and, after some days spent at Borrodale on the shore of Loch Nan Uamh, he raised his standard at Glenfinnan (above), at the north end of Loch Shiel. Today a viaduct (top and facing page top) carries the railway in a vast semi-circle round the head of Loch Shiel. A few miles from the head of Loch Shiel, Loch Eil (facing page bottom) stretches eastwards towards the prospect of Ben Nevis, at 4406 feet the highest mountain in Britain.

Top left: the island of Eigg, and (top right) Castle Tioram, on an island in Loch Moidart, which was originally a Jacobite stronghold until it was destroyed by its owner at the time of the 1715 Rebellion, for fear his enemies, the Campbells, would take it if he died. Above: the monument at Glenfinnan, erected in 1815 to commemorate the 1745 Rebellion. Mallaig (facing page bottom), the most important fishing centre in the west of Scotland, also serves the islands of Rhum and Eigg (facing page top), seen here from Sanna Bay. Bonnie Prince Charlie skirted these islands on his way to the mainland and Glenfinnan, on his escape from Culloden, on his return to the mainland and on his final flight to France.

On 16 April 1746, Bonnie Prince Charlie's Highlanders were defeated on Culloden Moor. On 27 April he crossed by open boat to the Outer Hebrides, where for two months he outwitted the military. Top left: the Standing Stones of Callanish, Lewis, about four thousand years old; (top right) Skigerska Harbour, Lewis; (centre left and centre right)

Stornoway, where the Prince tried in vain to get a ship in May 1746; (above left) the Lewis shoreline, and (above right) Castlebay, Barra, one of the southernmost of the Western Isles. Facing page: (top) Lewis Castle, Stornoway, built in 1840, and (bottom) Balallan, south of Stornoway.

Above: Horgabost Bay, Harris, and (top) a traditional croft, Baleshare, North Uist. It was from North Uist that the Prince embarked for Skye on 28 June 1746, disguised as the Irish maid of Flora Macdonald. He had just three other companions. Facing page top: Sound of Taransay, off the west coast of the 'Isle of Harris', which is actually not an island, but the southern part of the island of Lewis. Facing page bottom: East Loch Tarbert, where Bonnie Prince Charlie arrived on, and left, the island.

Bonnie Prince Charlie's escape party landed on the northwest coast of Skye (top). The following day, having changed out of his female disguise in a wood, the Prince walked to Portree. Here he said goodbye to the twenty-four-year-old Flora, who was promptly arrested on her way home. The Prince now crossed to Raasay and tried to contact MacLeod of Raasay, owner of the ancient stronghold of Brochel Castle (above), and he spent two fruitless days on that island. With one companion, the Prince then set out on foot for the south of Skye (facing page bottom), aiming for Strathaird, east of the Cuillin Hills (facing page top), to look for a boat. He found one at Elgol, and sailed for the mainland on 4 July 1746.

Top right: the Old Skye Crofters House, Luib, and (top left and centre left) the Cuillin Hills. Centre right: the Isle of Skye car ferry, and (above and right) the dramatic peaks of the Cuillins seen from Elgol. Facing page: the Cuillin Hills viewed from Loch Harport, and (overleaf) Glenfinnan's tangible reminder of the campaign of Bonnie Prince Charlie, who finally boarded a French ship and crossed the Channel in September 1746.

Left: King Robert I, better known as Robert the Bruce, looks out from Stirling Castle towards the field of Bannockburn. Top: Stirling Castle, the fortified gateway between north and south, and also a royal palace. Above: the palace block of Stirling Castle, built by James V. Facing page top: a dozen miles from Stirling, and high up in the Ochils, stands Castle Campbell, also once known as Castle Gloom, the lowland stronghold of the first Earl of Argyll. Facing page bottom: Alva Glen, at the foot of the Ochils, the site of ancient silver mines.

Top: Glasgow's River Clyde, where St Andrew's Roman Catholic Cathedral rises just beyond the bows of the S.V. *Carrick*, and (above) the façade of the city's Mitchell Library, a depository of over a million volumes, including the largest collection in the world of books on Robert Burns. Facing page: (top) a Glasgow skyline, epitomising the city's history: shipyard cranes mingle with steeples, banked by modern offices; and (bottom) S.V. *Carrick*, built in 1864 as a contemporary of the clipper *Cutty Sark*, and now the Glasgow RNVR Club.

Paisley Abbey (top), near Glasgow, was founded in 1163, destroyed by order of Edward I, and rebuilt after Bannockburn. Glasgow's City Chambers (above) were opened by Queen Victoria in 1888 – the interior is in Italian Renaissance style. Little remains now of the once-proud Clyde shipyards (facing page top). Facing page bottom: the Kelvingrove Art Gallery and Museum, which houses Britain's finest civic collection of British and European paintings.

Top: Edinburgh's night skyline seen from the direction of Calton Hill. Above right: the famous Military Tattoo on the Castle Esplanade, a feature of the Edinburgh Festival. Above left: the statue of Allan Ramsay, poet and wig-maker, in Princes Street Gardens, Edinburgh, and (facing page) the northwest aspect of Edinburgh Castle seen from Prince's Street Gardens. The fountain, with its faintly indelicate topmost figure, was made for the Paris Exhibition, and presented to the city in 1896.

Top: the Scottish National Gallery seen from the mound with, behind, the Royal Scottish Academy, built in 1826. Above: the Scott Monument, Princes Street. Facing page: (top) the monument to the philospher Dugald Stewart on Calton Hill, and (bottom) Dean Village, Edinburgh, a fascinating seventeenth-century survival.

Facing page: (top) Holyroodhouse viewed from Arthur's Seat, and (bottom) Abbey Strand, at the end of the Royal Mile, and the gates of Holyroodhouse, Edinburgh. Ramsay Gardens (top), by the Castle, stand on the site of the house built by Allan Ramsay for his retirement. Left: the memorial to Greyfriars Bobby, the devoted dog who kept watch over his master's grave for fourteen years, and (above) John Knox's House in High Street, Edinburgh. Overleaf: the Scottish National Gallery, the Scott Monument, Waverley Station and Calton Hill seen from the Castle. The tower on the summit is Nelson's Monument of 1807, and behind it is the National Monument, begun in 1822 but never finished.

Facing page: (top) the forecourt of Holyroodhouse, and (bottom) the Castle seen from Grassmarket in the Old Town, where a regular weekly market was held for over four hundred years. This was also the haunt of criminals and, until 1784, a place of public execution – a cross in the road marks the spot where many Covenanters were hanged. Top pictures: the new Waverley Market, off Princes Street, and (above) Princes Street Gardens, once the Nor' Loch, seen from the Castle walls. From the Palace and ruined Abbey of Holyroodhouse, the Royal Mile snakes up to Edinburgh Castle.

Hopetoun House (above), on the Forth, the home of the Marquess of Linlithgow, was built between 1721 and 1754 by William Adam and his sons. To the east of this house is Queensferry, named after Malcolm III's Queen Margaret, who used this route to travel between Edinburgh and Dunfermline. The railway bridge here (facing page) was built 1883-90 to withstand a wind pressure of 56lb per square foot in the light of the Tay Bridge disaster of 1879, though 30lb is regarded as adequate today.

Scotland's southwest is particularly noted as Robert Burns country. Top and above right: the house in Dumfries in which he died, now preserved as a museum. The ceremonial carving of the haggis (above left) on Burns Night is usually accompanied by a histrionic recitation of *Tam o' Shanter*. Still present today, sheep farms (facing page top pictures) were run by abbeys on the Border hills in the thirteenth century. Burns had a ewe, with two lambs, which inspired one of his earlier poems, *The Death of Poor Mailie*, though in fact the animal survived. Facing page bottom: Grey Mare's Tail, Moffat, a two-hundred-foot-high waterfall. The wild country around here was once a sanctuary for Covenanters.

Troon (top) lies on a narrow strip of land on the Ayrshire coast between Ayr, where in 1773 the young Burns boarded with his teacher John Murdoch, and Irvine to the north, where in 1781 he had a disastrous introduction to the flax-dressing trade. Above: Auld Brig o' Doon, which features in *Tam o' Shanter*, and (left) the Burns Monument, Alloway, erected in 1823. Girvan (facing page), a town which grew around a small fishing port, is at the mouth of the Water of Girvan, scene of some of the poet's dalliances.

Ailsa Craig (above), ten miles west of Girvan, is the haunt of seabirds and, until the 1950s, was the source of the best granite for the making of curling stones. Culzean Castle (top and facing page), built by Robert Adam for the Earl of Cassilis and dating mainly from 1777, was well-known to Burns and, as 'Colean', is mentioned in his poem *Halloween*. In 1946, the top floor of the central part was converted into a flat for the personal use of General Eisenhower, as a tribute to his wartime service in Europe on behalf of the Allies.

Castle Kennedy (facing page), by Stranraer, was built in 1607 and bought in 1677 by Sir John Dalrymple, who was later to become the first Earl of Stair. The gardens, originally laid out in the 1730s, are famous for their displays of azaleas, magnolias and rhododendrons. MacLellan's Castle (top), Kirkcudbright, dates from 1582, but has been a ruin since 1752. Threave Castle (above), on an island in the Dee by Castle Douglas, was built in the fourteenth century by Archibald the Grim as a Black Douglas stronghold, and destroyed by James II in 1455. Tradition has it that the cannon that did the damage was Mons Meg, now in Edinburgh Castle.

Smailholm Tower (above), by Kelso, is fifty-seven feet high, and a splendid example of a sixteenth-century Border peel tower. Sir Walter Scott knew it well, for he spent part of his childhood at nearby Sandyknowe Farm, and he made it the setting of his ghostly ballad, *The Eve of St John*. Facing page: the prospect of the Eildon Hills, known as Scott's View,

where he used to stop his carriage when he passed that way. At his funeral, the train of carriages was a mile long. Whether by accident or design, the procession halted when the hearse was exactly at this spot, and remained there for several minutes.

Facing page top: Abbotsford House, Melrose, built to Sir Walter Scott's specifications, where he entertained in style, and where he died. Today, many of his treasures can still be seen there. Melrose Abbey (top and facing page bottom) was founded in 1136, though much of what survives dates from the fourteenth century. In the fifteenth century it housed a hundred monks. It was destroyed several times, the last occasion on the orders of Henry VIII. Above: Leaderfoot Viaduct spans the River Tweed near Melrose.

Farther up the River Tweed is the town of Peebles (top), which Scott often visited and wrote about. It has other literary associations too. R.L. Stevenson lived there in his youth, as did John Buchan and his sister Anna (O. Douglas, author of Penny Plain). Dryburgh Abbey (above and facing page) was established in 1150 by the White Canons of the Premonstratensian Order as their first base in Scotland. It was destroyed by the Earl of Hertford in 1545. Sir Walter Scott lies buried in the north transept, and nearby is the burial vault of the Haigs of Bermonsyde, in which is the body of Field Marshal Earl Haig.

Facing page and top: Floors Castle, Kelso, which was designed in 1718 by Sir John Vanbrugh as the seat of the Duke of Roxburgh. Centre left: Kelso, and the elliptically-arched bridge built at the beginning of the last century by John Rennie. Left: the memorial presented to Coldstream in 1968 by the regiment which bears its name. Above: a piper, resplendent in richly-coloured tartan.

The road to the lighthouse (facing page bottom) at the southernmost point of the Mull of Galloway crosses two lines of earthworks dating from the first millenium B.C. Facing page top, this page and overleaf: Portpatrick, Wigtownshire. Between the seventeenth and nineteenth centuries, this town was an important element in the traffic between Scotland and the Scottish settlement in Ulster, and the main port of entry for Irish cattle, and for fugitive couples seeking marriage under Scottish law. The present harbour is what remains of an abortive plan by Sir John Rennie (son of the bridge builder) to turn it into a major port.

Facing page: (top) a distant prospect of the island of Arran, seen from the north, and (bottom) Arran's rocky shoreline. Tradition has it that Robert I landed on the north shore in 1307 after his voluntary exile on Rathlin. He kept watch at the point on the east coast known as Kingscross for the beacon from the mainland to tell him it was safe to cross to his native Carrick. Top: Brodick Castle, Arran, seat of the Dukes of Hamilton. The north wing dates from the thirteenth century. Above: a croft house, Boddam.

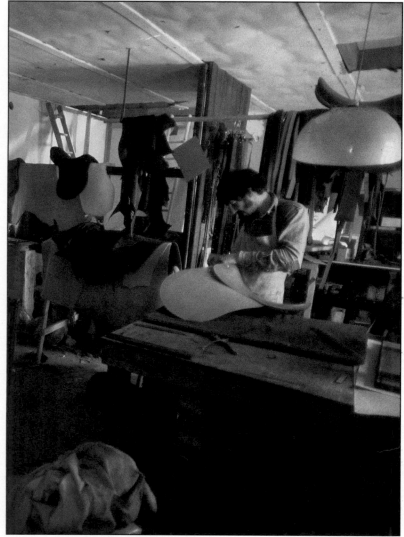

There is little industry in Arran, but traditional crafts are maintained (above and above right), and reflected in the Heritage Museum (top and right), Brodick. From the range called the Saddle, to the north of Goat Fell, a wild but negotiable path leads through Glen Sannox (facing page) back to the island's coast.

These pages: Rothesay, Bute. Bute has been a holiday resort since the early nineteenth century, when the Clyde paddle-steamers used to unload thousands of Glaswegians on the island, many of whom stayed in Rothesay. The town also has the distinction of being the site of Scotland's first cotton mill, established in the 1780s by James Kenyon. Thirteenth-century Rothesay Castle was a resort of Scottish kings, and the title Duke of Rothesay was conferred on the eldest son of the monarch from the time of Robert I. It is now held by the Prince of Wales.

The origin of the Highland Games (this page) probably lies in the contest organised by Malcolm III at Braemar to select the most effective warriors. Today's Games, which are held all over Scotland, involve piping, wrestling, tossing the caber – which can be up to twenty feet long – , putting the shot, throwing the hammer, and dancing. The Cowal Highland Gathering (bottom right), a feature of which is the 'March of a Thousand Pipers' – the thousand being an underestimate, takes place over two days at Dunoon. In the nineteenth century, Dunoon (facing page), in Strathclyde, was second only to Rothesay as a holiday resort.

At the end of the last century, Campbeltown (top left) was a base for 650 herring boats and thirty distilleries. Now there are few boats, and only two brands of malt whisky are made there. Rhunahaorine Point (top right), Kintyre, is the nearest spot to the island of Gigha to the west. Above: thirteenth-century Skipness Castle guards the north end of the passage between Kintyre and Arran. Tarbert (facing page bottom) not only commands the entrance to Loch Fyne (facing page top), but also the isthmus, which is the meaning of the Scots word ' tarbert'. Here Magnus 'Barelegs', King of Norway, crossed by ship, and here also Robert I, more legitimately, dragged his fleet on rollers 130 years later.

The Island of Gigha (facing page top) has traces of prehistoric occupancy, and between the fifteenth century and 1865 was owned by the McNeils, the Macleans and the Macdonalds. The much larger island of Jura, to the northeast, is noted for its peat. This is cut (top) in traditional fashion and laid out to dry (facing page bottom left). The population consists of some two hundred humans and five thousand deer, and the animals mainly inhabit the interior, where the country is virtually trackless. There is one village, and a distillery (above), established in 1880.

Oddly-shaped Islay is the southernmost Hebridean island. It is noted for tourism and its range of bird life, but its prosperity has depended on cattle (top left) and dairy farming, especially for the production of Islay cheddar and the mellower and creamier Islay Dunlop cheeses, and on whisky – there are eight distilleries, such as Bowmore Distillery (facing page centre left), and the peaty earth gives the malt a distinctive flavour. Above and facing page top: Port Askaig, entrance to Islay and the nearest port to Jura. Portnahaven (facing page bottom), the furthest point west, stands on the Rinns of Islay, a narrow bite of land which has seen many bloody battles between the Macdonalds, who originally settled it, and the Macleans, who were granted it by James VI.

Facing page top: Inveraray Castle, Loch Fyne, for centuries seat of the chiefs of Clan Campbell, the Dukes of Argyll. The present castle was begun in 1743, and its rich interiors, pictures and curios make it a great tourist attraction. Loch Riddon (facing page bottom) is an extension of the Kyles of Bute to the north. Younger Botanic Garden (top left), by Dunoon, is administered by the Royal Botanic Garden in Edinburgh, and contains a wide variety of trees and over two hundred species of rhododendron. Auchindrain Museum (top right), near Inveraray, preserves a nineteenth-century Highland communal farm. Above: Loch Eck, and (overleaf) Arrochar, Loch Long, with Ben Arthur – 'The Cobbler' – in the background.

The principal industry of the Isle of Seil, off Argyll, was its slate quarries. Quarrying started there at Easdale (above) in 1631, and continued until the sea flooded the area. Crinan (top and facing page bottom), on the Sound of Jura, is at one end of the Crinan Canal (facing page top), on which work began in 1793, in order that sailing ships bound for the Western Isles could avoid negotiating the Mull of Kintyre. The work suffered various disasters and financial crises, but eventually the present canal, redesigned and largely reconstructed by Thomas Telford, was opened in 1817.

This page: Oban Bay, where Dr Johnson and James Boswell landed from the Western Isles in October 1773, and in the town 'found a tolerable inn'. Facing page: Oban, seen from the bay, with the Mull ferry standing by for sailing. The town is the main link between the mainland and the Western Isles, and has been a popular resort since Victorian times. The circular edifice on the hill is known as 'McCaig's Folly'. It was built in imitation of the Colosseum in Rome by a local banker in the 1890s to give employment to masons and as a memorial to his family. It was never finished. Overleaf: Oban Bay, seen from the town, with the Isle of Kerrera and, beyond, the Firth of Lorne and the Isle of Mull.

Top and facing page: the Sound of Mull, which separates the northwest coast of the island from the mainland at Morvern, to which it was still attached about twelve thousand years ago, at the end of the last Ice Age. The volcanic lava which once covered Mull is now part of its soil, and helps give the island a rich variety of vegetation. Torosay Castle (above) was built in Victorian times in Scottish Baronial style. The gardens were laid out by Sir Robert Lorimer, friend and often-maligned business associate of Sir William Burrell. Right: a selection of locally-marketed delicacies.

Top and facing page top: Bunessan, Ross of Mull, lies on the road which culminates at the Sound of Iona, six miles further on. There is scarcely another road on this part of the island. Above: Calgary, Mull. The emigrants from this village gave its name to Calgary in Canada. Facing page bottom: Tobermory Bay, which, in Dr Johnson's view in 1773, 'appears to the inexperienced eye formed for the security of ships: for its mouth is closed by a small island, which admits them through narrow channels into a bason (sic) sufficiently capacious'.

Tobermory (top, and facing page) is the main port and the only town of Mull, and many of its cottages date from the eighteenth century. In 1588, a Spanish galleon, believed to be the treasure ship of the Armada, sought refuge in the harbour from the storm which had destroyed the fleet. Although the crew were made welcome by the inhabitants (who traditionally had too many inter-clan battles of their own to be concerned about England's wars), a local man, Donald Maclean, was later taken on board as a hostage. He got free, put a light to the powder store, and blew up the ship and himself. Above: yachting in the Sound of Mull.

Facing page top: Kilchurn Castle, Loch Awe and Ben Cruachan, a view which, in 1803, moved William Wordsworth to an outburst of impassioned verse. The castle was built in the fifteenth century by Sir Colin Campbell of Glenorchy, ancestor of the Campbells of Breadalbane. He was a Knight Templar who, caught up in the Crusades, was warned by a dream that his presence was required at home. He returned in disguise, just in time to stop his wife being married to a local laird, who had intercepted all his messages home. Top and facing page bottom: Loch Tulla. Traditional Highland cattle are descended from wild cattle mated with domesticated animals imported from Europe, and are characterised by shaggy hair and large horns (above).

Loch Etive runs east and then northeast from the Firth of
Lorne. There is no road on either side of it at its upper
stretch until, at Gualachulain, the loch gives way to Glen
Etive (these pages), which meets the Pass of Glen Coe.

This page: the head of Glen Etive in winter. Facing page: (top) cattle in Glen Coe, and (bottom) Scottish Blackface sheep. These are descended from a breed brought from England, and flourish especially upon heather moors. Their tough constitutions enable them to thrive on the hill and mountain slopes of Scotland.

Facing page top: Black Rock Cottage, Argyll. Top and facing page bottom: Buchaille Etive Mor, 'The Big Shepherd', towers over the road through Glen Etive. To the east of Glen Etive is the Black Mount (above), comprising seven peaks, each over 2,500 feet high. Overleaf: sunset over Loch Moy, from which the River Spean flows to Loch Lochy, passing Roy Bridge, scene in 1688 of one of the last inter-clan battles. Further down the river, at Spean Bridge, the first encounter of the 1745 Rebellion took place a few days before Prince Charles raised his standard at Glenfinnan. In this skirmish, a dozen apparently unarmed Highlanders put to flight two companies of troops.

Facing page top: Loch Moy, and (top and facing page bottom) Rannoch Moor, a vast peat bog described by the traveller Thomas Pennant in 1769 as 'truly melancholy'. With the Black Mount, it makes up one of the grimmest and bleakest regions of Scotland. In 1622 it certainly proved too much for John Scandaver, James VI's forester, who had been sent all the way from England by the King to catch a white hind which had been spotted to the south on the slopes of Corrie Ba. Scandaver and his companions saw the hind, but the weather was so awful and the going so tough that the forester eventually sat down and refused to go any further. Above: skiing in Argyll.

Facing page: Ardgour Mountains, seen from Loch Linnhe. Onich (top), on the east shore of Loch Linnhe, lies near the scene of the notorious 'Appin Murder' of 1752. Here, Colin Campbell of Glenure died after Stewart and Cameron lands had been forfeited to the Campbells following the 1745 Rebellion. James Stewart was hanged at the site of the crime, but his former guardian, Allan Breck Stewart, who was probably responsible, fled the country. This is the background to R.L. Stevenson's novel, *Kidnapped*. Above: the prospect across the loch to Corran, on the opposite side to Onich.

Top and facing page top: Castle Stalker stands on a tiny island in Loch Linnhe, with the hills of Mull in the background. The original castle was built in the thirteenth century. This one, a fine example of a tower house construction, dates from the fifteenth century and was owned by the Stewarts of Appin. James IV used to hunt from it. The castle, which has been re-roofed and restored for habitation, can be visited by appointment. Above: Loch Tulla and Stob Ghabar, one of the peaks of the Black Mount. Facing page bottom: Glen Lochy and the River Lochy.

These pages: Loch Lochy, beside which was fought one of the bloodiest and most pointless of clan battles. Here, in 1544, the Frasers and the Macdonalds took up arms over a slight which the chief of Clan Ranald felt he had suffered at the hands of his Macdonald kinsmen. The July day was so hot that the combatants threw off their plaids and fought in their shirts, and subsequently the place became known as 'The Field of the Shirts'. On the isthmus between Loch Lochy and Loch Arkaig is Achnacarry, birthplace of Donald Cameron of Lochiel, who was instrumental both in persuading other clan chiefs to join Bonnie Prince Charlie, and in dissuading the Prince from sacking Glasgow.

This page and facing page bottom: Fort William and Ben Nevis. The mountain is deceptive, since it has no real peak, and its mass makes it seem lower than it is. Fort William dates properly from 1665, when General Monk built an earth fort here. This was rebuilt in stone in 1690 on the orders of King William, from whom its name comes, and was one of the three military bases (Fort George and Fort Augustus being the others) built or strengthened in the aftermath of the 1715 Rebellion. Facing page top: the north face of Ben Nevis with modern Inverlochy Castle at its foot.

The red deer (top) is native to Scotland, and the stag is the largest British wild mammal. The stag's antlers are shed at the beginning of each year, and grow again by mid-July. Above and facing page top: Ben Nevis seen from the Caledonian Canal, which was opened in 1822 and is regarded as one of the most astonishing engineering feats of its time. It was originally suggested by James Watt, but Thomas Telford made the firm proposal and built it, thus enabling ships to avoid the north coast. There are twenty-nine locks along its length, eight of them by Banavie (facing page bottom). Overleaf: the lower falls of the Water of Nevis, which flows into Loch Linnhe.

The Caledonian Canal comprises twenty-two miles of man-made canal and lochs Lochy, Oich, and Ness. Facing page: (top) Loch Ness, and (bottom) the canal at Fort Augustus, where it enters Loch Ness. Castle Urquhart (top), Loch Ness, is one of the largest castles in the Highlands, and dates from the time of Alan Durward, 1st Lord of Urquhart and brother-in-law of Alexander II. It featured frequently in the struggles between the Lords of the Isles and the Crown. Fort Augustus (above), named after the Duke of Cumberland, was the first fortification to be built by General Wade in 1729. The village itself was originally known as Kilchuimen.

Eilean Donan Castle (these pages) stands on an island – latterly joined to the shore by a bridge – in Loch Duich, in a position which is both romantic and strategic. The original castle, now restored, was built by Alexander II to guard against, and as a deterrent to, Viking invasions from the west, and later belonged to the earls of Seaforth. In 1719 it was garrisoned with Spaniards by the Marquis of Tullibardine as part of an abortive Jacobite rising. It fell to three English frigates, which sailed up Loch Alsh from the sea and blew it apart.

Loch Carron is the next sea loch up the coast from Loch Alsh. Facing page: (top) the village of Plockton, at the entrance to Loch Carron, facing the mountains of Applecross across the loch, and (bottom) Loch Carron and Duncraig Hill. Plockton (top) is a popular yachting centre, as well as a holiday and retirement resort. On the other side of the Kyle of Loch Alsh, on the Isle of Skye, stands all that is left of Castle Moil (above), a name which means 'roofless castle'. It was once a look-out post against Vikings, and later a stronghold of the MacKinnons of Strath.

Loch Long (this page) – not the same as the one which meets the Firth of Clyde – joins Loch Duich by Dornie. Glen Shiel (facing page), down which the River Shiel runs to Loch Duich, was the setting for the defeat of the last remnants of the 1719 rising, on an old droving route from the north to the south. Dr Johnson and James Boswell passed along this road in the opposite direction in 1773, on their way from Fort Augustus to the coast, having – according to the Doctor – 'by the direction of the officers at Fort Augustus, taken bread for ourselves, and tobacco for those who might show us any kindness'. The Old Bridge of Shiel (facing page bottom) was the work of General Wade.

Rising almost sheer from Glen Shiel on its north side is the mountain range known as the Five Sisters of Kintail (top), seen here from Loch Duich. Above: Loch Quoich. Glen Affric (facing page top), to the east of Loch Duich, still retains its beauty and serenity, thanks to the determination and ingenuity of the North of Scotland Hydro-electric Board, one of whose major schemes has its power station at the head of this glen. Facing page bottom: Loch Cluanie, at the head of Glen Shiel.

Facing page top: deer in Glen Moriston, which links Loch Cluanie with Loch Ness, and through which Dr Johnson and James Boswell travelled from Fort Augustus. Facing page bottom left: netting cornstacks, (facing page bottom right) sheep-shearing, (top left) forestry, and (top right) cattle-raising – all old crafts which are still part and parcel of the Highland economy. Centre and above right: the Great Glen sheep dog trials and (above left) sheep farming. The Great Glen – or Glen More – runs from Fort William to Inverness, and was formed over three hundred million years ago by a massive geological movement. Overleaf: Inverness, where the River Ness joins the Moray Firth in sight of the Black Isle, the Cromarty Firth, and Easter Ross. Inverness was made a royal burgh by David I.

Top left: thatching in Cromarty. Victorian-built Inverness Castle (top) stands on the site of the stone fortress built by David I. Centre pictures and facing page top: oil rig construction and deployment in the Moray Firth. Left: Kessock Bridge between Inverness and the Black Isle, and (above) 18th-century Culloden House, now a hotel. Facing page bottom: Cromarty Bridge spans the Cromarty Firth.

Top left: Loch Shieldaig and village, Wester Ross. This sea loch contains an island belonging to the National Trust, the whole of whose twenty acres is covered with Scots pine. Gairloch (top right) is one of the few golf courses in the west Highlands. Above: Loch Torridon and Ben Liathach, which rises to 3,456 feet and is composed of red sandstone 750 million years old surmounted by white quartzite of almost the same age. Facing page: a Highland burn in Torridon, Wester Ross.

Top: Loch Torridon and Ben Alligin. Above left: sea fishing at sunset in Ardnair Bay, by Ullapool. Above right and facing page top: beach and sands at Gairloch, and (facing page bottom) the links at Gairloch.

Top: Ardmair Bay, (left) Rudha Reidh Point and the Stacks of Camas Mor, and (above) the bay in Loch Broom upon which Ullapool stands. Facing page: (top) Loch Broom and Ullapool, seen from the southeast, and (bottom) Ullapool itself. This town was planned, laid out and built as a fishing port by the British Fisheries Society in 1788.

Facing page: the River Inver, Sutherland, with Quinag behind. The river flows between Loch Assynt, where the Marquis of Montrose was betrayed, and Lochinver on the coast (above left). Above right: Loch Lurgainn, and Cul Mor, which rises to 2,787 feet. Top: Stoer Head lighthouse, on the Atlantic coast, Sutherland.

Scrabster (left and above), in Thurso Bay, Caithness, is the
ferry port for Stromness, Orkney. The Dounreay nuclear
power station is ten miles away, along the coast to the west.
Top: sheep farming near Altnabreac. Facing page: the sheer
cliffs and lighthouse at Dunnet Head, the northernmost
point of the mainland of Scotland.

Top: the signpost at John o' Groats, overlooking the Pentland – formerly Pictland – Firth, and the nominal end of the road from Land's End, Cornwall. John o' Groats himself was Jan de Groot, a Dutchman, who came to Scotland in the sixteenth century. As his eight descendants could not agree about their relative seniority, he is said to have built an octagonal house for them, with eight separate front doors, and an octagonal table for them to sit at. Above and facing page: the famous rock pinnacles of Duncansby Head, the true farthest point from Land's End.

Facing page: sunlight shows up the natural sandstone colour of the Duncansby Stacks. Just to the north of Lybster (top left), on the northeast coast, stands the remarkable prehistoric Hill o' Many Stanes, a series of uprights set in twenty-two rows, while the harbour of Dunbeath (top right), off the main road, contains a castle once besieged by

Montrose. Centre left: Highland outdoor ruggedness and (centre right) eighteenth-century elegance and comfort inside at Cromarty. Above left: the John o' Groats signpost, and (above right) uncompromising cliffs at Wick, the most northerly town on the east coast of Britain.

Brodie Castle (facing page top), near the coast east of Inverness, retains a weird variety of exteriors but, inside, refurbished from the seventeenth to nineteenth centuries, it offers traditional style, as well as a fine collection of paintings. A totally different example of restoration and preservation is the Sands of Forvie Nature Reserve (facing page bottom), on the coast just north of Aberdeen, the haunt of wildfowl in winter. Top: Slains Castle, between Peterhead and Aberdeen. This is the considerable ruin of a replacement by the 9th Earl of Errol of the structure destroyed by order of James VI. Its impressive eminence moved Dr Johnson to pronounce that he was happy to view storms from it. Above: Macduff, seen from the harbour of Banff.

These pages: east coast fishing ports. Facing page: (top) Gourden, Tayside, and (above and facing page bottom) Gardenstown, east of Macduff. Top: Stonehaven, the lower part of which, around the harbour, dates from the sixteenth century. The tolbooth, formerly a store for the Earls Marischal of Dunnottar Castle – a mile to the south – was used in the 1790s as a prison for Episcopal ministers, who still managed to baptise children through the barred windows.

Aberdeen, 'the Granite City', granted a royal charter by William the Lion in 1179, is still a major fishing port, and is the link between the mainland and the North Sea gas and oil operations. Top and above left: the bronze statue of William Wallace stands before His Majesty's Theatre of pink and white granite. The domed building to the left is the Church of St Mark. Aberdeen's Mercat Cross (above right) was sculpted by a country mason in 1686. The building behind it is a typical example of Scottish Baronial style. Facing page: (top) Aberdeen harbour, and (bottom) Aberdeen beyond the River Dee. The seven-span bridge was originally built in about 1620.

Top left: unloading the catch at Aberdeen. Ballater (top right), on the Dee, was the original railway station for Balmoral Castle, and still enjoys other royal cachets. Above: the lights of Aberdeen seen from the harbour. Craigevar Castle (facing page top), west of Aberdeen, is a six-storey, L-plan tower house completed in 1626. It has no later additions. Facing page bottom: Invercauld House, three miles from Braemar. It was from here or, more likely, from somewhere in the immediate vicinity, that the Earl of Mar called out the clans to start the 1715 Rebellion. He raised his standard at a spot now occupied by the Invercauld Arms.

Top: stags in Glen Clunie, and (above) ponies near Braemar. The complex nature of Balmoral Castle (facing page top), with the eighty-foot-high tower linking two wings, can be better understood when seen from the air. It is built of Invergelder granite, quarried on the estate. Prince Albert had the Castle equipped with a prefabricated iron ballroom, made in Manchester. Facing page bottom: the Old Bridge of Dee, on the road between Balmoral and Braemar.

Facing page: (top) the Old Bridge of Dee seen from the northeast, with Balmoral Forest beyond. (Bottom) Glen Muick, and the River Muick, which, observed Queen Victoria, 'falls in the most beautiful way over the rocks and stones in the glen'. The point at which the Muick joins the Dee is said to be the site of the castle which was the scene of the ancient ballad, *The Baron o' Brackley*. Top: the River Dee, past Braemar, and the Forest of Mar, which, Queen Victoria pointed out in1850, 'the Duke of Leeds rents from Lord Fife'. Above: the River Dee at the Linn of Dee, over which Queen Victoria opened a bridge in 1857.

The River Spey (these pages) starts high up in the mountains between lochs Laggan and Lochy, by the Corrieyairack Pass, through which Bonnie Prince Charlie went to meet Cameron of Lochiel during his final days in Scotland. It passes through Kingussie and Aviemore before entering Strathspey and finally flowing into the Moray Firth. On the opposite side of the Spey from Kingussie is Ruthven Barracks, where a few Jacobite survivors of Culloden regrouped, only to learn that their Prince had deserted them. Overleaf: Strathspey in winter.

Facing page: autumn in the Highlands, and (top) Christmas at Aviemore, which until after World War II was little more than a village and a railway station, with a limited summer holiday trade. The Aviemore Centre, the first of its kind in Europe, is now an all-year holiday, leisure, entertainment and sporting resort. Above: a view south over Loch Morlich to the Cairngorm Mountains.

The 'Ski Road' (facing page) from Aviemore to the Cairngorms crosses the Spey, follows the valley of the River Luineag, skirts Loch Morlich and becomes a chair-lift at Coire Cas. Farther up the chair-lift there is a plateau (top), beneath the summit of Cairn Gorm (4084 feet). Above: preparing the slopes for skiing.

Facing page: (top) a view north across the Tummel Valley, with Blair Castle and the Grampian Mountains on its far side, and (bottom) winter in Glen Clova. The bagpipes (top right), so indelibly associated with Scotland and Ireland, were in fact a Roman invention. Above: Perthshire Highland Games – a typical sight at a typical venue. Blair Castle (top left and overleaf), the tower of which dates from 1269, was visited by Edward III, Mary, Queen of Scots, and Queen Victoria, and occupied by Montrose, Cromwell, Claverhouse and the Duke of Cumberland, on which latter occasion it was unsuccessfully besieged by Prince Charles's general, Lord George Murray. It is the seat of the Duke of Atholl.

211

Facing page: Loch Tummel, (top) the view northeast across the Tummel Valley to Ben Vrackie, and (above) Loch Tummel with Schiehallion (3547 feet) beyond. On 30 August 1644, the Marquis of Montrose's army left Blair Atholl, immediately to the north, rounded Loch Tummel, and crossed the hills to Aberfeldy along the eastern side of Schiehallion. On Sunday, 1st September, he had, at Tippermuir, the first of his great victories. Overleaf: Pitlochry, famed for its Festival Theatre, with Ben Vrackie beyond. Loch Faskally, on the left, is an artificial loch, the end of a chain of lochs to the west and northwest which includes lochs Rannoch and Tummel and culminates at the Pitlochry Dam and Power Station.

These pages: Schiehallion, Fairy Hill of the Caledonians, seen from various vantage points. Top and facing page top: the mountain seen from the Queen's View, Pitlochry, on Loch Tummel. Though Queen Victoria passed this way several times on trips from Balmoral, the name is far older, and may refer to Mary, Queen of Scots. Above: Schiehallion beyond mist-covered Loch Tummel, and (facing page bottom) the mountain seen across Loch Rannoch, in which, in Sir Walter Scott's time, was believed to dwell a fairy water-bull which could only be killed by a silver bullet. Overleaf: the full splendour of Loch Tummel.

From Loch Tay, the river flows through Aberfeldy, under the bridge (facing page top) designed for General Wade by William Adam and opened in 1735. Facing page bottom: Aberfeldy along the floor of the Tay Valley, with Schiehallion in the distance. Aberfeldy was immortalised by Burns in his poem, *The Birks of Aberfeldy*. 'Birk' means 'birch tree', of which several can be seen in the foreground. By Dunkeld, farther down the Tay, lies Loch Lowes (top), which incorporates a nature reserve. A hill walk two miles from Dunkeld leads to the Hermitage (above), a folly, built originally in 1758, which overlooks the gorge of the River Braan.

Top and facing page top: contrasting aspects of Glen Shee, on the main road from Perth to Braemar. The village of Birnam (above), by Dunkeld, is best remembered as the site of Shakespeare's Birnam Wood, whose branches, in the play *Macbeth*, Malcolm (Canmore) orders his soldiers to hew down and bear before them, to hide their numbers from Macbeth, looking from his castle at Dunsinane. Dunsinane Hill lies fifteen miles away, to the southeast. Facing page bottom: the road from Dunkeld to Pitlochry.

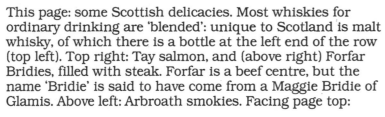

This page: some Scottish delicacies. Most whiskies for ordinary drinking are 'blended': unique to Scotland is malt whisky, of which there is a bottle at the left end of the row (top left). Top right: Tay salmon, and (above right) Forfar Bridies, filled with steak. Forfar is a beef centre, but the name 'Bridie' is said to have come from a Maggie Bridie of Glamis. Above left: Arbroath smokies. Facing page top:

Glamis Castle, seat of the Earls of Strathmore and Kinghorne, where Queen Elizabeth, the Queen Mother, spent her childhood. The turret in the foreground is part of one of the seven ancient gateways knocked down by Lancelot ('Capability') Brown, who redesigned the grounds in 1770. Facing page bottom: Glamis in autumn.

Glamis Castle (facing page and top left) was built between 1675 and 1687 for Patrick Lyon, 1st Earl of Strathmore, direct descendant of the son of Lady Glamis, who was burned for witchcraft in the time of James V. At its centre is a fourteenth-century L-shaped tower, some of whose walls are fifteen feet thick, thus giving reasonable rise to the rumour of a hidden chamber housing the Monster of Glamis. Top right: Wellington Square, Montrose. The steeple of the Old Church beyond was built in 1834. Above: Glamis in spring.

Top: the external aspect of Scone Palace dates from 1803, but the building incorporates parts of earlier palaces, as well as an abbey. The last coronation to be held at this traditional making-place of Scottish kings was that of Charles II in 1651. Above: the Tay Road Bridge, built in 1966, at Dundee and, beyond it, the Railway Bridge. The Tay Railway Bridge (facing page top) was begun in 1885 to replace the one that went down, with a train and 75 passengers, in the storm of 1879. The stumps of the old piers can still be seen beside it. Facing page bottom: Dundee, city of journalism, jute and marmalade, with the Tay Road Bridge in the background. Overleaf: the ancient city of St Andrews, with the ruins of the twelfth-century cathedral in the foreground and the famous golf-course beyond.

Facing page top: Elie, on the west coast of Fife. Crail (facing page bottom) and Pittenweem (top) are just two examples of Fife coast fishing villages and ports which still retain something of their medieval aspect. The stepped gable-ends, red tiles and whitewashed houses are especially typical. The curved tiles ('pantiles') are Dutch in origin, and came over as ballast in the little ships which carried coal, salt and other exports across the sea. Above: the Bannet Stane (Bonnet Stone) in the Lomond Hills overlooking Strathmiglo. Overleaf: Gleneagles Hotel and the most famous Scottish inland golf-course, home of the Scottish Open Championship.

Bass Rock (above), off the north Berwickshire coast, the other side of the Firth of Forth from Crail, was once a prison for Covenanters and also for Jacobites. Today it is a lighthouse base and the home of countless gannets and other seabirds. Facing page top: the harbour of North Berwick, beside which, on a narrow tongue of rock, are the remains of the Auld Kirk, in whose churchyard the North Berwick witches were alleged to have disported themselves while plotting the death of James VI. Facing page bottom: Longniddry Bay.

Facing page: (top) Carnbo, Kinross-shire, on the main road from Stirling to St Andrews, and (bottom) 17th-century Kinross House on the shore of Loch Leven. Kinnoull Hill (top), topped by a folly, overlooks the road from Perth to Dundee beside the Tay. Above: a view across the Tay in Perth, and (right) lantern-towered St Leonard's-in-the-Fields, beside the South Inch, Perth. Overleaf: the 'fair city' of Perth on the River Tay. On the left is Perth Bridge (1772), and between the two bridges stands the square tower and pale spire of St John's Kirk, much of which dates from the 15th century. Here John Knox launched the Reformation in 1559, sparking off an orgy of violence in the city.

These pages: four lochs in the Trossachs which have particular associations with Rob Roy MacGregor. Facing page: (top) a view southwest towards Ben Lomond over Loch Katrine, at the head of which he was born in 1671, and (bottom) Loch Arklet, by which he was married in 1693, in his bride's house at Corarklet. Top: Loch Voil, on the shores of which, in 1722, he successfully ambushed, and later released, a posse of law officers who were dunning rent from the MacIntyres of Invercaig. Above: Loch Earn, where, in 1716, he rescued from the law a member of Clan Gregor who had been arrested for illegally carrying arms.

Sir Walter Scott is credited with popularising the Trossachs region when he published his poem *The Lady of the Lake* (1810), which is set at Loch Katrine. Loch Lomond (these pages) and Ben Vorlich (facing page top) had in fact been popular with tourists for many years. One of the travellers in *Humphrey Clinker* (1770) by Tobias Smollett, who was born at nearby Bonhill, refers to 'the verdant islands that seem to float upon its surface, affording the most enchanting objects of repose'. It must be added that Dr Johnson, in 1773, was not so impressed with them: 'The islets, which court the gazer at a distance, disgust him at his approach, when he finds, instead of soft lawns and shady thickets, nothing more than uncultivated ruggedness.'

Facing page top: Loch Lomond, with Ben Lomond behind. After an all-night party at a mansion by the loch in 1787, Robert Burns and the male members of the gathering watched the sun rise over Ben Lomond, 'each man a full glass in his hand; and I, as a priest, repeating some rhyming nonsense'. After a short sleep, they spent the rest of the day 'on Loch Lomond', dined (very well) at Dumbarton and, on their way back, had a drunken horse-race with a Highlander, which predictably ended in a spectacular pile-up. Facing page bottom: autumn mist and romantic associations on Loch Lomond at sunrise. Above and overleaf: boats traditional and modern on Loch Lomond.

Top: Loch Lomond with Ben Lomond to the right, and (above) Loch Lubnaig. It was while walking here from Loch Voil at harvest time in 1803 that Wordsworth was moved to compose *The Solitary Reaper*. Scotland can boast only one lake, the Lake of Menteith; all the rest are lochs. A ferry runs from the Port of Menteith (facing page) to Inchmahome Priory, a ruined Augustinian house, founded in 1238. Here the infant Mary, Queen of Scots, was held in safety before her departure for France in 1548. Overleaf: Loch Achray and Ben Venue, and (following page) sheep in a highland wood in autumn.